This book is due on the last date stamp.
Failure to return books on the date due may result
in assessment of overdue fees.

FINES	.50 per day	

VERY SHORT INTRODUCTIONS are for anyone wanting a stimulating and accessible way in to a new subject. They are written by experts, and have been published in more than 25 languages worldwide.

The series began in 1995, and now represents a wide variety of topics in history, philosophy, religion, science, and the humanities. Over the next few years it will grow to a library of around 200 volumes – a Very Short Introduction to everything from ancient Egypt and Indian philosophy to conceptual art and cosmology.

Very Short Introductions available now:

AFRICAN HISTORY
    John Parker and Richard Rathbone
AMERICAN POLITICAL
    PARTIES AND ELECTIONS
    L. Sandy Maisel
THE AMERICAN
    PRESIDENCY Charles O. Jones
ANARCHISM Colin Ward
ANCIENT EGYPT Ian Shaw
ANCIENT PHILOSOPHY
    Julia Annas
ANCIENT WARFARE
    Harry Sidebottom
ANGLICANISM Mark Chapman
THE ANGLO-SAXON AGE
    John Blair
ANIMAL RIGHTS David DeGrazia
ARCHAEOLOGY Paul Bahn
ARCHITECTURE
    Andrew Ballantyne
ARISTOTLE Jonathan Barnes
ART HISTORY Dana Arnold
ART THEORY Cynthia Freeland
THE HISTORY OF
    ASTRONOMY Michael Hoskin
ATHEISM Julian Baggini
AUGUSTINE Henry Chadwick

BARTHES Jonathan Culler
BESTSELLERS John Sutherland
THE BIBLE John Riches
THE BRAIN Michael O'Shea
BRITISH POLITICS
    Anthony Wright
BUDDHA Michael Carrithers
BUDDHISM Damien Keown
BUDDHIST ETHICS
    Damien Keown
CAPITALISM James Fulcher
THE CELTS Barry Cunliffe
CHAOS Leonard Smith
CHOICE THEORY
    Michael Allingham
CHRISTIAN ART
    Beth Williamson
CHRISTIANITY Linda Woodhead
CLASSICS Mary Beard and
    John Henderson
CLASSICAL MYTHOLOGY
    Helen Morales
CLAUSEWITZ Michael Howard
THE COLD WAR
    Robert McMahon
CONSCIOUSNESS
    Susan Blackmore

For more information visit our website
www.oup.co.uk/general/vsi/

John Sutherland

BESTSELLERS

A Very Short Introduction

OXFORD
UNIVERSITY PRESS

OXFORD
UNIVERSITY PRESS

Great Clarendon Street, Oxford OX2 6DP

Oxford University Press is a department of the University of Oxford.
It furthers the University's objective of excellence in research, scholarship,
and education by publishing worldwide in

Oxford New York

Auckland Cape Town Dar es Salaam Hong Kong Karachi
Kuala Lumpur Madrid Melbourne Mexico City Nairobi
New Delhi Shanghai Taipei Toronto

With offices in

Argentina Austria Brazil Chile Czech Republic France Greece
Guatemala Hungary Italy Japan Poland Portugal Singapore
South Korea Switzerland Thailand Turkey Ukraine Vietnam

Oxford is a registered trade mark of Oxford University Press
in the UK and in certain other countries

Published in the United States
by Oxford University Press Inc., New York

© John Sutherland 2007

British Library Cataloguing in Publication Data

Data available

Library of Congress Cataloging in Publication Data

Data available

ISBN 978-0-19-921489-1

1 3 5 7 9 10 8 6 4 2

Typeset by SPI Publisher Services, Pondicherry, India
Printed in Great Britain by
Ashford Colour Press Ltd, Gosport, Hampshire

Contents

In reality there is no kind of evidence or argument by which one can show that Shakespeare, or any other writer, is 'good'. Nor is there any way of definitely proving that – for instance – Warwick Deeping is 'bad'. Ultimately there is no test of literary merit except survival, which is itself an index to majority opinion.

George Orwell, 'Lear, Tolstoy and the Fool'

List of illustrations

The publisher and the author apologize for any errors or omissions in the above list. If contacted they will be pleased to rectify these at the earliest opportunity.

Chapter 1
Definitions

Preface

Why read, or contemplate, with any degree of seriousness, less than 'good' (and sometimes downright bad) books – the Deepings of the literary world? Do they not belong in that category, contemptuously called in German, *Wegwerfliteratur*? – 'throw-away literature'? Why pick up what literary history so resolutely discards?

Any study of bestsellers confronts the same question as does the decaf, no-fat latte drinker in Starbucks: 'Why bother?' One justification, and the easiest demonstrated, is their (that is, bestsellers') interesting peculiarity. Like other ephemera of past times, bestsellers (even Orwell's despised Deeping) offer the charm of antiquarian quaintness. Where else would one encounter a line such as: 'I say, you *are* a *sport*, pater' ['Son' addressing 'Sorrell', on having been given a tenner 'tip' in Deeping's *Sorrell and Son*]. And, so short is their lifespan, that today's bestsellers become yesterday's fiction almost as soon as one has read them.

Looking back through the lists is to uncover delightful cultural oddities. Consider, for example, the top-selling (#1) novel of 1923 in the United States, *Black Oxen*, by Gertrude Atherton. Recall too that the discriminating reader of that year had James Joyce's

Ulysses, T. S. Eliot's *The Waste Land*, and D. H. Lawrence's *Aaron's Rod* to choose from.

Atherton's title is taken from W. B. Yeats ('The years like great black oxen tread the world'). The allusion signals grand literary pretension; pretension absurdly unmerited. None the less, the novel's theme was, for the time, both topical and sensational – rejuvenation. For humans, that is, not cattle.

The narrative opens in a New York theatre. A brilliant young newspaperman, Lee Clavering (a member of the city's elite 'top 400' families), is struck by a beautiful woman in the audience. Investigation reveals that she is facially identical with a young 'belle' of thirty years before, Mary Ogden. Miss Ogden married a Hungarian diplomat, Count Zattiany, and has never been heard of since. Speculation rages, but eventually the truth comes out: Ogden/Zattiany has been rejuvenated in Vienna by Dr Steinach's new X-ray technique. By bombarding a woman's ovaries at the period of menopause, the ageing process is reversible.

When news of the wonderful process hits the newspapers, 'civil war threatens'. And luckless Clavering finds himself in love with a woman old enough to be his mother. On the other side, he himself is obsessively loved by a flapper, Janet Oglethorpe, young enough to be his daughter, who drinks illegal hooch and attends 'petting parties'. The plot thickens, madly, thereafter.

It is nonsense – just as, medically, Steinach's X-ray miracle was nonsense. In 1922 Atherton herself had received the Viennese doctor's rejuvenation treatment. It seems, from publicity pictures, to have done little for her beauty. But tosh fiction and quack science as it may be, *Black Oxen* fits, hand-in-glove, with its period. And no other period.

However absurd it seems to the modern reader, Atherton's novel reflects, and dramatizes, contemporary anxiety about women's freedoms; as definitively as did *Bridget Jones's Diary* in the 1990s. The 1920s was the era of the 'flapper' – the perpetually young girl-woman. British women in this decade had, after long struggle, the vote – but only if they were over 30, after which the heyday in the female blood was conceived to have been sufficiently cooled to make rational political decisions. The cult of Dionysian youth – the 'be young forever or die now' aspiration – is more respectably commemorated in another novel of 1923, Scott Fitzgerald's *Beautiful and Damned*. It, too, made the bestseller lists, but much less spectacularly than Atherton: Fitzgerald was running a longer literary race.

Black Oxen, the top novel in the US in 1923, is inextricably 'of' its period. It could have been published 15 years later (as was Aldous Huxley's 'elixir of life' novel, *After Many a Summer*). But out of its immediate time-and-place frame, *Black Oxen* would have no more 'worked' than a fish out of water. Nor would it, in other days, have been what it was, 'the book of the day'. The day made the book, as much as events of the day made newspaper headlines in 1923.

This hand-in-glove quality is inextricably linked with the ephemerality of bestsellerism. A #1 novel may be seen as a successful literary experiment – as short-lived as a camera flash, and as capable of freezing, vividly, its historical moment. If (to paraphrase Coleridge) one saw *Jonathan Livingston Seagull* ('Jesus tripping') wandering wild in Arabia, one would shout: 'hippy seventies!' (with the possible addition 'dude!'). If Bulldog Drummond blundered, dinner-jacketed, into one's living room, his 'man' Denny in close attendance with pint tankard, furled brolly, and pistol, one would recognize the clubland thug as a time traveller from the early 1920s.

The great literary work may be, as Jonson said of Shakespeare, 'not for an age but for all time'. The reverse is, typically, the case with the 'best' bestsellers. They are snapshots of the age.

An American kind of book

There is no advance in the merchandising of books – from the feuilleton (newspaper serial), the dime novel, through the pulp magazine, the mass-market paperback, the webstore, and, of course, the bestseller and its apparatus – that America has not pioneered and brought to perfection.

America was peculiarly suited for the development of a popular fiction industry and its most dynamic manifestation: the bestseller. As a democracy, America came into being at the same time as the rise of the novel. With their revolutionary proclamations, the new state's founders enshrined rights to freedom of expression and the pursuit of happiness. Bestsellers aim to supply those commodities.

There was, unlike in Europe, no tradition of state control over literature or its makers. Commercial control, via privilege or monopoly, is similarly alien to American laissez-faire literary culture. Apart from a brief period in 1915, America has not imposed any system of retail price maintenance, such as Britain's Net Book Agreement: a trade pact (deemed illegal under American anti-trust law), introduced in the 1890s and abolished in the 1990s, devised to discourage 'underselling', or competitive pricing. 'Let 'er rip' has always been the American commercial motto.

America has enjoyed (and typically invented) the world's most advanced printing, transport, and communication technologies. Most importantly, in its formative 19th-century phase, until April 1891, the American book trade was wholly unfettered by any adherence to protocols of international copyright. It was in the happy position of being able to plunder mature European – principally British – literary cultures at will and without sanction.

For the first hundred years of its existence, the flag of the American book trade was the Jolly Roger. And most systematically plundered was British literary property. The effect is easily demonstrated. F. L. Mott's 'Overall Best Sellers in the United States', his monograph on the subject, uses for its survey the calculus of 'a total sale equal to one per cent of the population of the continental United States for the decade in which it was published'. Mott lists, by this finicky reckoning, 124 bestselling 'American' novels, in the period 1776 to 1900. Of those, 74 are actually British in origin; 15 mainland European (mainly French); and a mere 55 native products.

Huckleberry Finn: a case study

'All modern American literature', pontificated Ernest Hemingway, 'comes from one book by Mark Twain called *Huckleberry Finn*.' And, one may add, beneath its vernacular idiomatic surface – as American as Pike County – great chunks of Twain's perennially popular novel come from pirated foreign sources. The narrative is worm-holed with un-American popular fiction.

When, for example, Tom sets up the preposterous scheme to spring Jim from the shed in which Aunt Sally has imprisoned the luckless slave, the young rogue cites – what else? – *The Count of Monte Cristo*. As he explains, to a sceptical (and notably less literate) Huck:

> It don't make no difference how foolish it is, it's the *right* way – and it's the regular way…look at one of them prisoners in the bottom dungeon of the Castle Deef, in the harbour of Marseilles, that dug himself out that way; how long was *he* at it, you reckon?'
>
> 'I don't know.'
>
> 'Well, guess.'
>
> 'I don't know. A month and a half.'

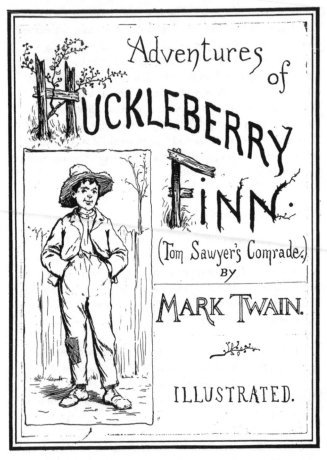

1. *Huckleberry Finn*, the original edition of 1884, illustrated by E. W. Kemble

'*Thirty-seven year* – and he come out in China. *That's* the kind. I wish the bottom of *this* fortress was solid rock.'

But it is the Wizard of the North, rather than Dumas, whose romance underlies Twain's realism. When he raises his gang, at the outset of the story, Tom does so with the burning cross of *The Lady of the Lake* (a narrative which, incidentally, also furnished the Ku Klux Klan with much of their ritual and symbolism). 'Walter Scott' is the name of the meaningfully wrecked steam boat which sets up the collision between the hero's romanticism and the real world, where real hurt happens.

Twain believed that Scott – the most pirated novelist of the century – had poisoned the American soul, and was responsible for the Civil War. It is curious speculation, even for Twain, that subscription to international copyright might have preserved the country from the bloodiest war in its history.

The American sales hot-house

Freed of the necessity to originate its own bestselling fiction, the American book trade's energies tilted towards selling the product – and selling to a public which was, across society, more literate and book-hungry than Britain's. It was a hot-house in which new sales techniques could, and did, emerge.

The British book trade, with a smaller economic base, a more organic (London) literary world, and a smaller (island-sized) reading public, tilted more towards origination. And, given hefty start-up costs for the commodity, the British book trade cartelized to maintain a sky-high sales price for fiction. A new novel cost more in the 19th century than at any period before or since. A three-volume first edition of, for example, Mrs Humphry Ward's *Robert Elsmere*, under the Smith Elder imprint, would have cost the consumer in 1883 a guinea and a half (not far short of £100 in modern currency). Assuming, of course, that any consumer were rich or mad enough to disburse that much (there was, the Victorian joke went, *one* person who *once* bought a three-decker – but no one, dammit, could remember the fellow's name).

The legions of English readers who devoured Mrs Ward's story and suffered, along with the hero, the agonies of religious doubt, borrowed their volumes (a volume at a time, typically) from a circulating library. By thus 'renting' the novel for a short period, the vast purchase cost was minimized. The publishers and middlemen got their profit (3,500 three-volume sets of *Robert Elsmere* were sold in six months), and, with demand stoked sky-high by the library buzz, the booksellers could wait for the cheap (but, at 6s, hardly dirt-cheap) reprints in a year or so (60,000 cheap copies were sold). Everyone was happy. No apple carts were upset. Reading matter flowed out, serenely, to the reading public; a golden stream of cash flowed serenely back, diverging profitably into library, bookseller, and publisher's pockets (at the end of the food-chain, authors themselves might get something).

Meanwhile, in New York, a few weeks after the book went on sale in Hatchard's in Piccadilly, *Robert Elsmere* could have been bought for a quarter (25c) in any number of Broadway outlets. It is estimated 100,000 copies were sold within the year in America, and getting on for a million in three years, all at fractions of British prices. America's was a buying, not a borrowing, book culture. And more hectic with it. The unfettered laws of supply and demand drove the price down until, at the financial nadir, the pious English lady's ultra-pious fictional tract was being given away, free, with bars of soap; on the principle, presumably, that cleanliness was next to godliness. From the hundreds of thousands of copies of her novel sold in the US, Mrs Ward got not a plugged nickel.

The licence to plunder the seasonal British crop ended when America, finally and reluctantly, signed up to international copyright law in 1891. Mrs Humphry Ward was among the first to benefit, with a huge American advance (£7,000) for her 1894 novel *David Grieve*. But old habits and practices died hard. American books remained markedly cheaper than in Britain for the consumer. Ward's 1894 bestseller sold, new, for 31/6d in the UK, and for $1 (an eighth of the price) in the US. The differential, a hangover from the era before the 1891 Chace Act, persists to this day. A hardback American bestseller is still marginally easier on the pocket than its UK equivalent.

There are other hangovers from the period in which the American book trade so prodigiously reaped where it had not sown. Particularly in British crops. Nowhere is the 'relationship' more 'special' than in popular fiction. This can be readily demonstrated by comparing the British preponderance with other groups who have, historically, made up a large part of the American population. Despite, for example, huge immigration from Germany, and its cultural impact on American life in the early 20th century, only one novel from that country has ever made it to the coveted #1 spot in that country: namely Erich Maria Remarque's *All Quiet on the Western Front* (1929). After World War II, Remarque's similarly anti-war (and, as was felt in Germany, anti-German) novel *Arch of Triumph* made the top ten in 1946. A handful of other novels translated from German have figured in the lists: Lion Feuchtwanger's *Jew Suess* (1926); Vicki Baum's *Grand Hotel* (1931); Hans Fallada's *Little Man What Now?* (1934), *The Forty Days of Musa Dagh* (1936), and his 'Lourdes Story', *The Song of Bernadette* (1941). Patrick Süskind's *Perfume* (1986) was the last German novel to figure at all prominently in the American top ten.

'Isak Dinesen' (Karen Blixen) was in the top ten in 1935 with *Seven Gothic Tales*. Her fellow Scandinavian, the Finn Mika Waltari, established a more substantial place in the lists 20 years later with *The Egyptian* (1950, and again in 1955, with the movie adaptation of the novel), *The Adventurer* (1951), and *The Wanderer* (1953). Annemarie Selinko, a German refugee long resident in Denmark, may be thought also to qualify in this national group. Her historical novel, *Desirée*, was a bestseller (tied in to the movie about Napoleon, starring – grotesquely – Marlon Brando) in 1954.

Russian fiction first made an entry in the American lists (less for the author's origins, than its setting in war-torn China) in 1942 with Nina Fedorova's *The Family*. Boris Pasternak's *Doctor Zhivago* shared the top position, week in week out, with his (Americanized) compatriot Vladimir Nabokov's *Lolita* in 1958. Alexander Solzhenitsyn, as the 'thaw' in the Cold War took hold, made the lists in 1972, with *August 1914*.

French-originated bestsellers are notably absent, represented solely by the two *rive gauche* novels Françoise Sagan's *Bonjour Tristesse* (1956) and Simone de Beauvoir's *The Mandarins* (1958). Both were boosted by the mid-1950s cult of French *nouveau vague* film. The sole Italian representative to have made any dent on the lists is di Lampedusa's study of an aristocratic Sicilian dynasty, *The Leopard* (1960) – generally regarded as one of that country's very greatest literary achievements. Australia has Coleen McCullough's bodice-ripping *The Thorn Birds*, #1 title in 1977.

Despite Spanish now being a second language in border states, only three Hispanic-originated novels have ever made it to the top ten. Ibanez's *Four Horsemen of the Apocalypse* was the #1 title in 1919 (a year still in post-trauma from the truly apocalyptic World War I). The philosopher George Santayana's *The Last Puritan: A Memoir in the Form of a Novel* made the top ten in 1935, and is regarded as the finest *Bildungsroman* (portrait novel) ever to do so. Laura Esquivel's *Like Water for Chocolate* was intermittently, in the weekly lists, #1 in 1993.

This handful of titles excepted, anything other than British titles are absent from the upper reaches of the American bestseller lists. The following is a breakdown, by place of national origin, of the 1,000 novels representing the decades' top ten titles, 1900 to 1999.

Decade	US	British	Other
1900–09	86	14	0
1910–19	76	23	1
1920–29	71	28	1
1930–39	68	28	4
1940–49	85	11	4
1950–59	82	11	7
1960–69	83	16	1
1970–79	71	27	2
1980–89	84	16	0
1990–99	94	6	0
Totals	800	180	20

The fluctuations suggest, unsurprisingly, a greater penetration by the British product in the first half of the century (104 of the total 180). There is a notably sharp chauvinistic swing towards American fiction in the 1990s.

Anni Mirabili

Throughout the 20th century, although there was an overall drift towards the home product in the US, there were regular resurgences, or extraordinary clumps, of Britishness in the American lists. The so-called *Annus Mirabilis*, 1924–5, for example, saw the publication of P. C. Wren's *Beau Geste*, P. G. Wodehouse's *Jeeves*, and Edith M. Hull's *The Sons of the Sheik* – all of which clustered at the top of the 1924 charts. The following year saw *Soundings*, by A. Hamilton Gibbs (the #1 novel in America that year), Margaret Kennedy's *The Constant Nymph* (#2), Michael Arlen's *The Green Hat* (#5), Rafael Sabatini's *The Carolinian* (#9), and A. S. M. Hutchinson, *One Increasing Purpose* (#10). *Sorrell and Son*, published in England in 1925 and in America a year later (where it made #1), set Warwick Deeping on what was to be a ten-year-long domination of the American charts. So powerful was Britain's performance that there were jeremiads about it in the American press bemoaning the decline in national literary prowess.

This colonial shadow lies heavily across the greatest 'American' book of 1925, *The Great Gatsby*, in which the hero does a 'Yank at Oxford' stunt to win over Daisy, the woman he loves. Dreaming spires and Jay Gatsby are 'great'; Kansas and James Gatz (his 'true', farm boy, identity as we learn late in the narrative) ain't great. Now recorded as the most studied novel in American high schools, *The Great Gatsby* did not make the 1925 list. As was noted earlier, Fitzgerald was running a longer literary race.

One can perceive other years throughout the century when the British content bulged significantly. The 1925/6 *annus mirabilis* is attributable to the warm connections forged by wartime alliance 1917–18. The Americans came over here: British fiction went over there. Something similar is detected in 1940 – a year in which America was 'neutral', but nonetheless, in her heart, side by side with her transatlantic cousin. The bestselling novel of that first year of the European war, rather bizarrely, was Richard Llewellyn's story of life, hardship, and indomitability in a Welsh coal-mining village, *How Green was my Valley* (filmed, even more bizarrely, with a Hollywood cast, in 1942; it turned out that even Llewellyn – despite his name – was about as Welsh as Jimmy 'the Schnoz' Durante; but this did not prevent the film sweeping the Oscars that year).

The third title on the 1940 American bestseller list was *Mrs Miniver*, by Jan Struther. It had begun as a series of newspaper articles in the US, in 1939, commemorating British pluck and 'we can take it' coolness under fire. It was the special relationship bestsellerized. According to Winston Churchill, Struther had done more for the anti-Fascist cause than a flotilla of battleships. The old warhorse none the less wanted his liberty ships from his friend Franklin Roosevelt.

Other good, if not wonderful, years pop up regularly. In 1937, A. J. Cronin's *The Citadel* came in at #3, Virginia Woolf's *The Years* at #6 (surely the result of enthusiastic reviewing in high places), and Somerset Maugham's *Theatre* at #7.

In 1977 the top title was Tolkien's posthumous codicil to his 'Rings' epic, *The Silmarillion*, with John Le Carré's novel about dishonourable spooks, *The Honourable Schoolboy*, at #4, and John Fowles's semi-autobiographical *Daniel Martin* at #10. Given the runaway success of Tolkien (a million-seller in hardback), over half the bestsellers sold of the top ten had British authorship blazoned on their American title pages.

Bestsellerism and anti-bestsellerism

Despite these impressive conjunctions of material, one major institutional factor in the 20th century served to differentiate, radically, British and American bookselling practices. Britain in the 1890s had introduced the 'Net Book Agreement' (NBA) – a measure that kept the country's book trade in line for a hundred years. Effectively, the NBA compact forbade, on pain of collective trade boycott, the selling of books at less, or more, than the sale price posted on the wares by the publisher. No reduction, or surcharge, in price for these 'net' (that is, net-price) books – which invariably included new novels – could be offered by any retailer, however many copies were bought or wherever the copies were bought. The NBA also, effectively, suppressed the growth of the book clubs which in America (with the Book of the Month Club and the Literary Guild) disseminated millions of hardback fiction titles annually, at fractional cost, to the reading population. Book clubs took off in the UK only decades later, in the 1960s.

In Britain, for most of the 20th century, a single copy purchased in the corner shop in John O'Groats, or Land's End, would cost the same as each of a hundred copies bought from Hatchard's in Piccadilly. The effect was to create a low-pressure, 'civilized', or 'carriage trade' ethos. This was further enhanced by British resistance to any 'sale or return' facility for the retailer. In America, a major bookstore could order 1,000 copies of some novel and – if the thing died on the shelf – return 999 for full refund. In Britain, once ordered, the books were yours. It made for cautious ordering by bookshop managers.

America, after a brief flirtation with retail price maintenance during World War I (which US courts promptly banned as 'cartelization'), never bought into the Net Book idea. It was disdained as radically un-American: socialistic, almost. Discounting on purchase price – either in shops or book clubs – served as gasoline to the bestseller list's flames. And it was only after the abolition of the NBA in the UK in 1995 that the two national systems converged – to the degree that they are now, in their largest formations, supra-national.

2. Newspapers reported an industry in turmoil as the Net Book Agreement was dismantled in 1995

Are HarperCollins, or imprints like Heinemann and Secker & Warburg, sheltering under the Random House umbrella, British, American, neither, or both? Send your answer to London, New York, Sydney, or Toronto. Or Berlin – since the parent Random House is now German-owned. (John Murray, Walter Scott's and Jane Austen's publisher, is now French-owned: something that would baffle both of them, fiercely patriotic as they were during the Napoleonic Wars.) The author Ken Follett, who was born and educated in Britain, sells very many more copies of his books in the US than in the UK, and his bestsellers, such as *Code to Zero* (#1, 2000), have American settings and characters. Where does he belong? Perhaps the answer will be found in his papers, deposited at Saginaw College in Michigan.

For a hundred years, from the 1890s until the 1990s, British book culture (along with its European counterparts) was inherently inimical to the idea of the bestseller and disdained, entirely, any official 'lists'. This American barbarism, as it was thought, distorted customers' buying habits. Discriminating readers 'browsed', like ruminant beasts chewing the cud in an English meadow; they did not 'stampede' like maddened cattle across the Great Plains.

The high sales pressure associated with American styles of bestsellerism cramped, it was felt, the range of bookshops' stock. Beneath mountainous piles of whatever 'the book of the moment', worthy books struggled to be seen. Books did not 'compete' with each other – they were 'different', as a successful 1960 British legal defence of retail price maintenance insisted (successfully; the Net Book Agreement was judged 'legal'). No one ever said, as of books, 'where baked beans are burned, men are burned'. Why, then, sell books like baked beans? Or so the British book trade felt.

As a result of this cultural resistance, the first reliable lists did not arrive in the UK until the mid-1970s, when the *Bookseller* began assembling them for the trade, and *The Sunday Times* began making them available to the reading public. Over following years they became an established feature of the British book world, which has in other ways accommodated to American high-pressure salesmanship – more so after the abolition of the NBA in 1995, and the evolution of the traditional high street bookstore into something virtually indistinguishable from the American hyperstore. In the US, it is Barnes and Noble, Borders, and Amazon.com; in the UK, Waterstone's, Borders, and Amazon. co.uk. And one increasingly sees the same novels at the top of the two countries' bestseller lists.

Terminology

Any kind of book can be a bestseller. Even, in my wildest dreams, this Very Short Introduction. But ever since bestseller lists first appeared, the term has primarily attached itself to works of fiction – those jam tarts for the mind, as William Thackeray called them. In what follows, reference is exclusively to the bestselling novel, literary sweetmeats.

The actual term 'bestseller' is first recorded as coming into use in 1902, some seven years after the first 'lists' were introduced. The term was, from the first, a misnomer. 'Best' is a superlative. If one is being precise, as in the film *Highlander*, 'there can only be one'. Whether the Bible, Shakespeare, or the *Highway Code* is a moot point.

But, as the lists make clear, week by week, there is always more than one bestseller, so called (up to a couple of hundred in the latest trade lists), and – one may be confident – next year's bestsellers will probably be bigger and better bestsellers. The next decade's certainly will be.

When we use the term 'bestseller', we buy into book trade (white) lies. It is commonly, nowadays, called 'hype' or 'spin': mendacity in a good cause – that cause being the sale of more and more books to more and more people. The correct term would be 'better sellers', or 'new books that are currently doing well until something newer comes along'. When the bestseller first appeared, at the tail end of the 'gilded age' when publishing still prided itself on being a profession for gentlemen, the preferred term for what we now call bestsellers was 'books in demand'. Until the 1920s, with works such as A. S. M. Hutchinson's phenomenally popular *If Winter Comes*, the British book trade referred to 'big sellers'. Semantically preferable as such terms might be, these were too tame for the aggressive commercial mood of the 20th century.

'Fast-seller', it is often suggested, would be another preferable label. It is the pace of sale, not the ultimate total of sales, that defines a bestseller. *The Pilgrim's Progress*, less than page-turning as it may be as a religious thriller, has outsold *The Da Vinci Code* many times over. But it has done so during half a millennium of devout readership. A century hence, Mother Church will surely survive. Leonardo's picture will still draw its crowds in the Louvre. And – one may confidently predict – Bunyan's allegory of the Christian life will still be read, if only for its timelessly chaste prose. But Dan Brown's anti-Catholic fantasia? Probably not – other than by literary archaeologists – and certainly not for its prose. Over the period 2003 to 2006, *The Da Vinci Code* 'outsold' *The Pilgrim's Progress* only in the sense that it sold (briefly) faster. Which of the two, then, merits the description 'bestseller'?

Over every bestseller list there should be a *carpe diem* inscription: books of the day and for the day only. Read them while ye may, then toss them away.

The Number One *New York Times* Bestseller

DAN BROWN

THE DA VINCI CODE

'Fascinating and absorbing...
A great, riveting read. I loved
this book' **HARLAN COBEN**

3. *The Da Vinci Code*: 'bestseller'

OXFORD WORLD'S CLASSICS

JOHN BUNYAN
THE PILGRIM'S PROGRESS

4. *The Pilgrim's Progress*: bestseller?

The literary bestseller

One must enter a cautionary qualification. Bestsellers, as a category, are wholly unpredictable as to content and literary quality. No one, even those whose instincts are sharpened by a working life in the book trade, can say, for certain, which way the market will jump. Fewer publishers would go bust if they could. Most novels will fail even to cover their production costs, of that one can be sure. But any novel, and any kind of novel, can triumph; even, from time to time, literary novels. This uncertainty, and its occasionally surprising consequences, can be put in the form of a quiz:

Q. What do Mickey Spillane and George Orwell have in common?

A. They both sold 6m copies of an individual novel, written in the same year.

Q. Where would one find *August 1914* and *Jonathan Livingston Seagull* side by side?

A. On the 1973 bestseller list, as the top two titles.

Q. What do the following have in common: *Doctor Zhivago*, *Anatomy of a Murder*, *Lolita*, *Around the World with Auntie Mame*?

A. Over the year 1958 they were, at various times, all the bestselling novel of the week and the top four (in the order above) in the final, annual, round-up.

One could put together a very respectable educational curriculum from the bestseller lists. Or, alternatively, a scathing indictment of utterly degraded British and American popular taste, as Q. D. Leavis did, in 1932, with *Fiction and the Reading Public*. Any work of fiction, as the charts indicate, can qualify: whether high literature (such as E. L. Doctorow's *Ragtime*, #1 American bestseller in 1976), brutal pulp (Spillane's *I, The Jury*,

#1 paperback in 1946), or cynically conceived schlock (Erich Segal's *Love Story*, in 1970).

The top spot may be occupied by a title posterity will come to regard as a 'classic', such as Harper Lee's *To Kill a Mockingbird*, alongside a work of near pornography, such as Harold Robbins's *The Carpetbaggers* (the novel which, in February 2007, Myra Hindley credited as the inspiration for her and Ian Brady's infamous child murders). Chalk and cheese, both titles are listed as 1961 bestsellers. That, and the fact that they are generically 'fiction', is the only point of contact they have.

As a rule of thumb what defines the bestseller is bestselling. Nothing else. There may be rhythmic recurrences, over long periods, as fashions wax and wane, but to look for significant patterns, trends, or symmetries is, if not pointless, baffling, as will be discussed in Chapter 3.

Chapter 2
The modern scene

Definitions: continued

The invention of the printed codex in Western Europe in the 15th century coincided with the arrival of cheap-to-manufacture paper from the East. With this new technology, reading material could be manufactured massively and instantaneously for societies now preconditioned to receive the product by higher levels of literacy, bourgeois prosperity, and urbanization.

No longer did a codex require months of laborious penmanship to create a single copy. The problem now lay less with the speed with which the bookseller could manufacture the commodity (as was the case with the scriptorium) but the speed with which he could bring his books to market.

Books are, with coinage, the first article of mass production, historically. Without the minting press and the printing press – and the currencies of wealth and of ideas they put into circulation – the modern world would not have happened. One has no way of knowing, but Master Caxton's works of fiction, Malory's *Morte d'Arthur*, and Chaucer's *Canterbury Tales* were probably the top sellers in our first bookseller's very mixed list.

Sales mania

The ability of the printing press to manufacture books in instantaneous over-supply answered, and inflamed, a reciprocal appetite in the consumer – what one might call 'cultural impatience'. The bestseller feeds on mania: the 'I want it now' urgency. Now means this minute: next week is too late.

The history of bestsellerism can be summed in images such as customers jostling each other like players in a rugby scrum to buy copies of Scott's *Rob Roy* in 1819, tearing off the brown paper packaging to get at the book within, and devouring the opening pages in the London street. Or stevedores, shouting to the incoming ships, as they steamed into New York Harbor, 'Is Little Nell dead?' Or queues forming outside bookshops hours before opening time to buy the newly acquitted 'Lady Chat' on 13 November 1960 ('would you like it in a plain paper bag?', the shop assistants politely enquired – acquitted Lawrence's novel may have been: thoroughly respectable it was not).

A recent manifestation, 'Pottermania', has touched unprecedentedly manic levels. On 19 July 2005, the sixth instalment of J. K. Rowling's saga of boy-wizardry was released, on the stroke of midnight.

The books had been bonded like contraband. As the witching-hour approached, crowds gathered in high streets and outside bookshops throughout Britain. Many were decked out in pointed hats with broomsticks (as, wretchedly, were shop assistants kept from their beds by Pottermania). When the doors were thrown open, purchasers were no more selecting Rowling's book from the thousands available elsewhere in the store than a crowd, in a burning cinema, would pause on their rush to the exit to buy popcorn. Over a million copies of *Harry Potter and the Half-Blood Prince* were sold over the country's counters in 24 hours, and as many by the electronic bookstores.

5. Pottermania hits Kuala Lumpur, on the day of global publication of the fifth book in the series

Stampede selling

Bestsellers inspire such Gadarene episodes – although few as picturesquely as that triggered by Rowling's fiction. Why, when reading is so private an activity, should people want, so simultaneously, the one 'book of the day'? There are so many books (and so many days) available to the discriminating reader – a much larger variety than, say, films, television programmes, or live theatre performances. The novel-reader's choice is dizzyingly extensive. Amazon's new and used title catalogue grows weekly. With a couple of keystroke clicks and a number inscribed in plastic, the reader has a choice of some two million fiction titles, and more every year. There are so many novels that even if one dedicated one's whole life to reading them, and doing little else, one would – novel in hand on one's deathbed – only have scratched the surface of the fiction mountain.

Why, then, are so many million citizens reading the one, or the top ten, or (in recent times) the top hundred novels at any one time? Why are they not browsing rationally among the vast array of reading matter on offer to them? Or, put another way, if it's popular fiction they want, why are they not reading the bestsellers of ten, twenty, or a hundred years ago?

With genre products, it is less mania than loyalty. Readers tend to be either brand-loyal to a particular category (science fiction, romance, horror) or to a particular author (see the myriad websites around, for example, Stephen King or Anne Rice). Given the fact that the essence of fiction marketing is variety, and constant renewal of stock, this loyalty too is as irrational as that mobilized to sell one-off blockbusters. But, where there is irrationality, there is money.

Make it new

The bestseller is, arguably, the purest form of narrative, in that it is always 'new'. It is the most novel, and continuously renovated, variety of novel. Once in print, like Dracula in the morning sunlight, the bestseller's novelty quickly fades, making way for its newer successor.

Since the arrival of the bestseller lists in the US, only a tiny handful of novels has held the top spot for two years: and then, typically, because they are year-straddlers, published in autumn or winter. Those novels are: *The Good Earth* (1931–2), *Anthony Adverse* (1933–4), *Gone with the Wind* (1936–7), *Jonathan Livingston Seagull* (1972–3), *The Da Vinci Code* (2004–5). *The Celestine Prophecy* hovered near the top for three years, 1994–6, no one knows why.

It would be hard to discern any stand-out literary quality or characteristics to account for what is, in this hyper-accelerated context, Methuselean longevity. But it is plain that one would, in the normal course of events, no more read (for pleasure) a previous decade's bestsellers than last week's newspaper (for news). If proof is required, compare the bookshelves of the Oxfam charity shop with the 'top sellers' display in the next-door Waterstone's.

The top of the bestseller list is, culturally, the slipperiest of poles. There are, technically, two such poles: hard- and paperback. The first, since the books are spit-new, tends to be the slipperier. Few titles survive in either list more than a few months; most dip in (briefly) and out (forever).

It is tempting to see the bestseller in a polar relationship with 'canonical' fiction – the titles, that is to say, which feature in such 'classic reprint' series as Oxford World Classics or Penguin Classics. But even their select contents are subject to tides (albeit slower tides) of fashion. In the 1970s and 1980s, Anthony Trollope rode very high: every one of his massive 47-strong fictional *oeuvre* was in print (some in as many as five separate, budget-priced imprints). In the 1990s, Wilkie Collins's 'sensational' fiction overhauled the Chronicler of Barsetshire. Other shifts in taste could be perceived, and though slower than those seen in the bestseller charts, no more than with them was the canon a fixed and enduring thing.

Demographic factors clearly come into play. Syllabus-makers in the educational system tend to occupy their career places for 40 years – exercising a stabilizing effect over that period. New reading publics, with subtly different tastes, will reach adult literacy levels every 15 years or so. Death thins out the cohort at the other end. The composition of the total reading public changes over time. For practical purposes, it is more sensibly seen as less a monolithic thing than a fluid constellation of many smaller interest groups. A 50-year-old product of the 1970 education system may well take a volume of George Eliot on vacation with him. A 30-year-old product of the 1990 education system a novel of (then more fashionable) Mary Elizabeth Braddon. Sixty-year-old women readers will probably be less likely to read chick-lit than their grand-daughters, and their respective male partners less likely to read Andy McNab than John Le Carré.

Regional and generic bestseller lists have been devised. The book trade has not yet (although it surely will) come up with age- or generation-specific bestseller lists.

Revenant bestsellers

Even harder than staying at the top of the slippery pole for over a year is the 'comeback'. Very few novels indeed have ever returned to the bestseller list having lost their position there for more than a year. And, where occasional comebacks have been achieved, there is invariably some easily identified extraneous factor. The first novel to have managed this difficult double-dip trick was *The Robe*, Lloyd C. Douglas's melodramatic re-telling of the gospel story, which was first a #1 bestseller in 1943 and again in 1953. *The Robe*'s resurfacing after a ten-year absence was entirely attributable to the lavish 1953 Cecil B. DeMille film adaptation.

In the UK, John Galsworthy's 1920s *roman-fleuve*, *The Forsyte Chronicles*, was similarly revived by the 1967 televisation which enthralled the nation. Oprah Winfrey's book club endorsement made Pearl S. Buck's *The Good Earth* and John Steinbeck's *East of Eden* superannuated bestsellers decades after they had first figured in the lists. Most amazingly, George Eliot's *Middlemarch* was, for a month or two, the bestselling fiction paperback in the UK in spring 1994, on the strength, again, of a massively popular television dramatization by Andrew Davies.

In the absence of such extraordinary circumstances, like the snows of yesteryear, once the bestseller's brief season is gone, it is gone for good. For those of a curious disposition, this relates to one of the bestseller's perennially fascinating aspects. Why was 'everyone' in 1925 reading *Sorrell and Son*, or *The Cardinal* in 1950, or *Wheels* in 1971, when those books are so irretrievably out of print now that one must go to a copyright library to dig up copies?

One can attempt to answer the puzzle by revisiting those years, recovering what one can of the *Zeitgeist*, and pondering the coincidence of factors – ideological, social, cultural, commercial – which led to the novel's hitting that particular historical mark. The bestseller, regarded in this light, is a literary experiment that works, for its time. But, typically, only for its time. Regarded carefully, it can be seen to fit the period that gave it birth as a tailored glove fits the hand.

Given their diversity, bestsellers can, but often don't, repay close literary-critical attention. But for what they tell us about the host society in which, briefly, they came good, bestsellers are among the most informative literary-historical evidence available to us.

Paperback bestsellers

The reprint novel, as an adjunct to the new commodity, originated with the 'Standard Novels' series, devised by Henry Colburn and Richard Bentley in the 1830s. What this enterprising pair of London publishers invented was a two-tier system in which the expensive new book (at a whopping guinea and a half) would take the risk and return higher margins of per-copy profit. The reprint novel (at 6s) would put back into circulation a smaller number of 'surefire' titles – those that had succeeded in the expensive form – and generate, per item, lower (but safer) returns.

This two-tier pattern survives to the present as hard- and soft-cover issue. In game theory terminology, it's a maxigain (hardback)/miniloss (paperback) dualism. Relatively rarely does a fiction title succeed in mass-market paperback form that has not been a success in the more expensive form.

The mass-market paperback originated around the same period, in the 1930s, in the UK and the US, but in markedly different national forms. In the UK, the mass-market paperback pioneer was Allen Lane, with his Penguin Books, launched in 1935. After a quickly aborted experiment with Woolworth's 3d and 6d department stores, Lane's stylish reprints established themselves in conventional bookshop outlets. Penguins were, from the first, paperbacks that sold like hardbacks, and in many cases were an even more respectable imprint. For an author, to be 'Penguined' was a mark of high merit.

Lane eschewed pictorial covers throughout his long career as Britain's leading paperback publisher. He thought them vulgar. His editors were instructed to concentrate on a superior quality of paper, design, and type to create commodity fit for the finest reprint fiction. And for Allen Lane.

In America the mass-market paperback pioneer was Robert de Graff. His strategy was less to embed his product in the traditional bookstore than to circumvent that outlet entirely. De Graff's 25c 'Pocketbooks' were, essentially, 'drugstore' paperbacks. They had eye-catching illustrative covers, newsprint-quality paper (one notch up from the toilet roll), and, typically, slapdash typography. They were designed to sell less like books (items of civilized furniture) than short-life magazines. And not, necessarily, the more respectable kind of magazine.

Since the 1960s, and the subsequent 'paperback revolution', the British and the American mass-market paperback have assimilated in terms of appearance and marketing style. American paperbacks have gone somewhat upmarket; British paperbacks have come somewhat downmarket.

Mass-market paperbacks remain books that are, generally speaking, beneath critical notice – especially fiction. They are not customarily reviewed, and rarely have pride of place in bookshop window displays. This ostracism is particularly regrettable with 'genre fiction', where serious critical evaluation is relegated to the fanzine or, more recently, the webzine.

'Critical opinion' is, by contrast, important and often vital to the success or otherwise of hardbacks.

Chapter 3
Fields and lists

Covering the field

It would rupture the capacity of a Very Short Introduction
(or even a very long one) to deal with even the output of a single
week's bestsellers. There are, as Ken Gelder suggests in his
monograph on popular fiction, two approved ways of dealing with
the subject and compressing it into discussability.

One strategy is taxonomic. This offers a kind of *catalogue
raisonné*, usually chronological, invariably highly selective, from
(say) *Robert Elsmere* to Robert Ludlum with accompanying
commentary – critical or sociological – and some statistics
thrown in to stiffen the mix. Gelder has his doubts about this
approach.

The method approved by Gelder is to 'map the cultural
field' – using the tool of contemporary literary theory, derived
principally, in his case, from Pierre Bourdieu. Gelder discards the
term 'bestseller' as problematic, preferring 'popular fiction'. This
term invokes, for Gelder, the prime consideration of *intention*.
The motives of the (would-be) writer of 'literary fiction' are
distinctly different from those of the (would-be) popular novelist.
The literary novel can, of course, be popular – a bestseller
indeed – but that is not where it starts.

The root problem is the same with both approaches described by Gelder: namely, the sheer numerousness and variability of the object ('the bestseller/popular fiction') under inspection. There is so much of it. The undergraduate who studies English Literature at honours level for three or four years at university will, in their final examination, be expected to demonstrate proficient knowledge of around 50 texts. Ever since the first degree courses in the subject were launched in the 19th century, this has always matched the fixed, and immutable, quantum of classical literature, which has survived to us from ancient Greece and Rome (a corpus whose total content can be contained on two 3.5-inch floppy disks).

Bestsellers offer the equivalent of a new canon every year. If one wanted to do a *Tristram Shandy*, it would, quantitatively, require three years' hard work to study one year's output conscientiously – even if one could work full-time at it.

The bestseller/popular fiction awaits its Linnaeus. Mapping the field will not be a very short task, or something that can be achieved by any one scholar, however assiduous. The great Swedish botanist did not have to deal with his plant world expanding faster than science could come up with names for its specimens. Pragmatism, and Jack Hornerism (sticking in the thumb and pulling out some plum), remain the soundest critical methods.

Is it, in fact, a 'list'?

Placement on the bestseller list identifies the bestseller as such. But the list itself is a peculiar kind of tabulation. It is not, for example, the same as the sales figures recorded in a publisher's ledger. Nor is it the same as digitized compilations like Bookwatch, which have been made possible by ISBN identification and point of sale monitoring – modern technological innovations that can chart the patterns, tides, and surges of book purchase down to single unit accuracy. Or the PLR register, which lists (for the purpose of fee payment) borrowings from public libraries.

The bestseller list is as much ahead of the event as behind it, and exists to *create* sales as much as to record them. It is dynamic, not passive; an engine, not a catalogue. It belongs in the publicity rather than the accounting department of the book trade.

If a novel achieves that coveted #1 spot, it will, for a certainty, enjoy a sales spurt as a result of that achievement. This kind of dynamic chart was first developed, in its most effective form, in popular music, where 'number one' is so valuable a property that unscrupulous impresarios have been prepared to bribe outlets with payola to get it. So too, from time to time, have publishers in the US been suspected of storming those outlets used to compile the lists with suborned purchasers. Increasingly, publishers are willing to buy premium display places on shop floors (or web store sites), and discount savagely, less to sell copies than to get the title into the top ten, or 20, or 50. Once there, the momentum will carry them onwards to still higher sales.

The lists (II)

The practice of systematically identifying, and listing, certain books as noteworthy for the speed and volume of their sales – and absolutely nothing else – began with the American monthly magazine *The Bookman*, and its editor, Harry Thurston Peck, in 1895.

Peck's magazine was the first to list a selection of new titles 'in order of demand' – that demand being measured by units of sale. The first lists comprised some ten titles (all novels) a month, with annual round-ups. At this inaugural point, in the 1890s, the fiction bestseller lists of the *Bookman* were dominated ('colonized') by British titles. Seven out of the ten top novels of 1895 were British in origin.

There was, as has been noted, a historical reason. Until 1891, America declined to sign up to international copyright regulation. As a result, the country's publishers were free to help themselves to whatever new British works took their fancy, free of charge, which they enthusiastically did.

The earliest recorded use of the compound noun 'best-seller' occurs in 1902. In 1912, the American trade magazine *Publisher's Weekly* began issuing a bestseller list, which has been authoritative ever since. A year later, the trade magazine began dividing bestsellers (customarily ten per week) into fiction and non-fiction – although the term 'bestseller' automatically evokes (as here) a certain kind of novel.

Since 1913, further subdivisions have emerged: notably hardcover and paperback, children's books, 'how to' manuals. Regional variations and even outlet variations can be registered and fed back into a central monitoring database for analysis. One of Waterstone's London flagship shops, that by University College London (formerly Dillon's University Bookshop) will, for example, have very different patterns of sale from the other flagship outlet in Piccadilly (formerly Simpson's). Epos (electronic point of sales) systems for the capture of data have made retailing apparatus infinitely more sensitive. Gloves fit hands ever more snugly. It is now, literally, possible to identify 'books of the day', or even of the hour.

Bestseller: title or author?

Agatha Christie (1890–1976), only twice in her 56-year career, came close to heading the annual bestseller lists, with the *Curtain* (#3 in 1975) and *Sleeping Murder* (#2 in 1976, the year of her

6. Agatha Christie

death). Both novels were written years earlier and intended to be published posthumously, as her legacy.

Since, as a World War I nurse in 1916, she wrote (while on short leave) *The Mysterious Affair at Styles* (1920), Christie's scores of detective stories have sold, at rough calculation, two billion copies worldwide (she is, for example, the best-ever-selling novelist in France, outdoing even Georges Simenon). Her novels still sell – year in, year out – in their millions. *The Guinness Book of Records* nominates her as the bestselling (the *very* bestselling) novelist ever.

The Case of Christie (to adapt the favourite title formula of one of her disciples, Ellery Queen) highlights a crux in the use of

the term 'bestseller'. Christie, the 'Queen of Detective Fiction', is
indisputably a bestseller, although her books, item by item, have
hardly ever been bestsellers by the strict definition of placement
on the lists. Margaret Mitchell and Harper Lee, by contrast,
each published only one novel: *Gone with the Wind* and *To Kill
a Mockingbird* are bestsellers by virtue of their #1 placings in
1936 and 1961, respectively. But one would not call these novels'
authors 'bestsellers'. So faint, indeed, are the public images of
these works' makers that many schoolchildren for whom Lee's
novel is required reading assume the author to be male.

It is particularly in genre fiction, where authors typically
produce their wares in multitudes, that the issue is trickiest.
Edgar Wallace, the anointed 'King of the Thrillers' in the first
half of the 20th century, was a bestseller – although, with the
exception of *The Four Just Men*, very few of his works ever
sold overwhelmingly. *In toto*, however, he merited his crown.
Wallace – year in, year out – turned out the same kind of book
as efficiently as Nuffield produced Morris motor cars, using a
Dictaphone and a team of stenographers to do so.

Barbara Cartland – with 600-plus novels to her name in the
copyright library – also mass produced her wares with the
assistance of a regiment of amanuenses (all fluffily clad in
trademark pink, one would like to think). Not one of her books
merits the epithet 'bestseller', although she certainly does.

Obviously, literature generated, on a factory scale like so many
fictional widgets, will have generic similarity. Read one Cartland
Regency romance, and you've read them all. Read one Wallace
thriller, and you will have a good idea of what's coming next. But,
like alcoholics, one was too many but a thousand not enough for
the brand-loyal corps of readers.

It is not quite a case of Tweedledum's 'bestsellers mean what I
mean them to mean', but one needs constantly to qualify the term

by reference to the shifting polarities of producer and product, author and title, one-off and genre.

Are there cyclical patterns?

In his study of the subject, *Making the Lists*, Michael Korda suggests that there are cyclical patterns in the American bestseller. Like the Laffer curve in economics, or boom/bust sequences in the housing market, the same kinds of book recur over time with meaningful regularity in the bestseller lists.

The Korda thesis may be tested (and, arguably, confirmed) by reference to 'religious bestsellers' – novels that take on themselves the Miltonic task of explaining the ways of God to man. In which years does one see this variety of bestseller outselling all else, as the book of that particular year, in America? As best they can be tabulated, the following are the years in which newly released religious titles, in which Christ himself or his disciples figure, outsold all other novels in the US:

1855   *The House of David*, Joseph Hold Ingraham
1880   *Ben Hur*, Lew Wallace
1896   *Quo Vadis*, Henryk Sienkiewicz
1897   *In His Steps*, Charles M. Sheldon
1942   *The Big Fisherman*, Lloyd C. Douglas
1943   *The Robe*, Lloyd C. Douglas

The Tim La Haye and Jerry Jenkins *Left Behind* fictionalization of the Book of Revelation (which has already yielded numerous #1 titles) concludes with the Redeemer as a prominent character in *Kingdom Come* (2007). Alas, more fictional than prophetic.

It is hard to see any chronological rhythm or historical significance in these recurrences. There may, of course, be accidental factors: catastrophes, world wars, mass immigration, the shifting tides of secularism and evangelism. Demography may be involved. But one's final conclusion is sheer bafflement: beyond, that is, the one fact that formulae do seem to come and go. Although, if one takes a very long view, interesting recurrences can be observed.

When, in *Jurassic Park* (1990), Michael Crichton blatantly rewrote Conan Doyle's *The Lost World* (1912), was it conscious? And was the fact that both novels were, in their respective times, hugely popular fortuitous? The fact that Crichton (a writer who has always been generous in his acknowledgements) followed up *Jurassic Park* in 1995 with a novel called *The Lost World* suggests that he knew exactly what he was doing in taking a scenario out of the great stock-pot of (pot-boiling) bestsellers and recycling it for a public who would, collectively, have forgotten all about it.

Eight years after World War I came Bulldog Drummond – a two-fisted English gentleman of the old school taking on world conspiracies, in the shape of his great adversary Carlson, and winning. Eight years after World War II comes James Bond, fighting his Dr Evil, Blofeld. When creating 007, Fleming studied Sapper's (H. C. McNeile's) thrillers. But is the postwar interval a factor in the phenomenal popularity of the ultra-English superheroes?

There is no copyright in ideas, scenarios, or narrative gimmicks. Even highly original (seeming) bestsellers can often be found, consciously or unconsciously, to be formed by what in the book trade is called 'me-tooism', or what, in more censorious areas of intellectual life, would be called plagiarism. And, within this zone of free-for-all, there is much recycling. Whether there are large cyclic patterns is a provocative but at this stage hard-to-prove thesis.

At some point, it may be possible to map out bestsellers in more rational ways than we currently heap them (in 'lists') or loosely corral them (with terms like 'melodrama', 'romance', 'crime', and so on); for the moment, we can't.

Ever better sales

The crunching sound of numbers, particularly sales figures, is the background music to bestsellerism. Contemplating those numbers, one can see that thresholds have heightened markedly over the decades – although not always in a straight line.

In general, what used to be a bestseller would, in terms of sales, not qualify nowadays. *Anthony Adverse*'s selling 600,000 copies over four years in the late 1930s was seen as phenomenal. Seventy years later it would be nothing special. In fact, Hervey Allen's blockbuster was overtaken, barely after it had dropped from the lists, by *Gone with the Wind*, which sold a million in a year. Now the top five novels in some years in America (and some titles in the UK) can match that without requiring calls to *The Guinness Book of Records*.

Regarded over the century or more of its accurately recorded existence, one can see the bestseller as the product of a machine which enlarges annually and whose output grows proportionally. Enlarged populations, enlarged wallets, enlarged literacy, and new cultural technologies are contributory factors, but do not entirely account for the growth. Vertical rationalization is a crucial factor – smoother cooperation (and agglomerated ownership) between different media. The machine has become more efficient at doing what it does. There have been advances in retailing, which has become ever more sophisticated, with the arrival of webstores, 'chaining', and book hypermarkets.

Whatever the explanations, following the best-recorded line – that of the American fiction bestseller in the 20th and 21st centuries – the trajectory is ever upward: bigger sales and faster sales.

Examining *Publisher's Weekly* records in 1945, Alice Payne Hackett determined that the all-time bestseller, to that date, was Charles Monroe Sheldon's Christian epic *In His Steps* (1895), with cumulative sales (boosted by the 'What Would Jesus Do?' movement which it founded) of some 8 million over 60 years. *Gone with the Wind* (1936) had, by 1945, clocked up 3.5 million.

Undertaking a parallel exercise in 1965, Hackett calculated that Grace Metalious's steamy saga of sex in a New England suburb, *Peyton Place* (1956), had sold almost ten million copies in under ten years. In 1975, Hackett discovered that with the paperback revolution of the late 1960s, there were now novels, like Mario Puzo's *The Godfather* (1969), Peter Blatty's *The Exorcist* (1971), and Erich Segal's *Love Story* (1970), that had sold ten million or more in five years.

With these long (if ever-shortening) slabs of time, Hackett was necessarily lumping together first and reprint forms of the novels to make a general point about acceleration and massification. A sharper figure emerges if one takes maximal, first-year sales of (American) bestsellers across a century. Single factor tables, especially in a field as complex as literature, have their dangers, and one would not want to draw too much from the following peak figures. But in terms of trend, they surely witness to an inexorable pattern of growth:

1900:	250,000	Mary Johnston, *To Have and To Hold*
1910:	250,000	Florence Barclay, *The Rosary*
1918:	500,000	Vicente Ibañez, *The Four Horsemen*
1928:	240,000	Thornton Wilder, *The Bridge of San Luis Rey*
1936:	1,000,000	Margaret Mitchell, *Gone with the Wind*
1945:	868,000	Kathleen Winsor, *Forever Amber*
1951:	240,000	James Jones, *From Here to Eternity*
1958:	421,000	Boris Pasternak, *Doctor Zhivago*
1968:	300,000	Arthur Hailey, *Airport*

1969:	418,00	Philip Roth, *Portnoy's Complaint*
1972:	1,800,00	Richard Bach, *Jonathan Livingston Seagull*
1976:	250,000	E. L. Doctorow, *Ragtime*
1977:	1,000,000+	J. R. R. Tolkien, *The Silmarillion*
1978:	851,000	James Michener, *Chesapeake*

After the 1980s, the 200,000 threshold was nothing special. In 1983, for example, the top 25 new novels all passed that mark. In 1989, 63 novels passed the 100,000 mark. By the 1990s, one million first print runs were routine for novelists such as Jean Auel, Stephen King, Tom Clancy, John Grisham, and Danielle Steel. In 1986, 'the year the hardcover went mass market', the top three titles (Auel's *The Mammoth Hunters*, Michener's *Texas*, and Garrison Keillor's *Lake Woebegon Days*) all sold a million or more in their first year, in expensive hardback form. In 1991, *Scarlett*, Alexandra Ripley's sequel to *Gone with the Wind*, was, like its original, the #1 novel of the year and sold over twice as many copies, breaking through the two million barrier. In 1994, Robert James Waller's *The Bridges of Madison County* doubled even that, by selling well over four million. Since that time, a million in the first year is as unexceptional as 200,000 had been during the previous decade.

As impressive as the sales, or the advances paid to authors (in the tens of millions for King, Grisham, Steel, and Jeffrey Archer in the 1990s and thereafter), was the cover price the American consumer was prepared to pay for the new hardback blockbuster. James Clavell's *Noble House*, for example, the #1 novel in the US in 1981 (Clavell, incidentally, was a British writer), cost the customer, before discount, $19.95 for its 1,200 pages. Clavell went on to get an advance of $5m for his next novel, *Whirlwind* (1986).

One can hazard some hypotheses for the peaks and troughs in sales. Films in the 1920s and early 1930s, and television in the 1950s and 1960s, arguably challenged, and for a while depressed, first-year, hardcover, bestseller sales. So did the explosive growth of the mass-market paperback ('I'll wait for the cheap version') in the 1960s. But in the 1980s (the 'me' decade) something along the lines of an 'I want it now, I won't wait' imperative seems to have kicked in. Contributory factors were the growth in literacy, the growth in population, and increasingly sensitive, digitized market research and advertising. Digitization, in addition to rationalizing, cheapened the whole arc of production, distribution, and sale, from the author's word processor to webstore, rendering the hardcovered book that beloved Victorian thing, 'a cheap luxury'.

Chapter 4
The American bestseller

Prehistory

The work conventionally regarded as the first American bestseller (although its author was born and raised in England) is Susannah Haswell's sub-Richardsonian tale of female tribulation, *Charlotte Temple* (1794). The tear-jerking narrative has a New York setting and there are some 200 known American editions over the succeeding century. Haswell's novel left an indelible, primal mark on American sentimental romance – something which would flower, dramatically, in the 'feminized fifties' (i.e. 1850s).

America in the early 19th century had its rival 'Author of *Waverley*' in the shape of James Fenimore Cooper, who cannily nativized Scott's formula with leather stockings instead of kilts, pistols instead of claymores, tribes instead of clans – blending Caledonian tints with the traditional, and popular, 'Indian Tale' (with Scott's romance providing one of the deeper roots of the early 20th-century 'western').

The influence of Scott's *Rob Roy* can also be detected in Daniel P. Thompson's *The Green Mountain Boys* (1839), a freebooting tale of land-grabbing and bloody feud in Revolution-period Vermont (America's 'Highlands'). Thompson's novel ran through some 50 editions in 20 years. As with Cooper, the 'frontier' was, at this stage, still the Eastern seaboard.

There was also North and South. If Walter Scott, as Twain (half-seriously) asserted, 'caused' the Civil War by an overdose of romance administered to the American people, Abraham Lincoln took a different view. He was keen to shake the hand, the President said, of 'the little woman who started a great war'. Whether or not Harriet Becher Stowe, rather than the Harper's Ferry raid, was the 'cause', *Uncle Tom's Cabin* (1852) was indisputably the first bestseller to break entirely the Scott or Dickens mould in America (although echoes of Mrs Gaskell's social problem novel, *Mary Barton*, are distantly heard – plantation slaves replacing Manchester wage slaves).

Stowe's was also the first American novel to be a runaway bestseller in Britain, levelling up cross-Atlantic inequities a (very) little. The London publisher, George Smith, was gratified, on his journey to work, to perceive all six people in his first-class carriage reading *his* (pirated) edition of Stowe's novel. It was some consolation for the wholesale Yankee pirating of his *Jane Eyre*, five years earlier.

In America, Stowe's fictional tract sold in unprecedented numbers – the demand for 10,000 copies a week wore out Jewett's printing presses while stoking up Boston's abolitionist fires to white heat. Never had the *power* of popular fiction been demonstrated so clearly. Not even by Dickens. Stowe had forged what would become an enduring link between the American bestseller and the American social conscience. 'What an accursed thing slavery is!', her novel exclaims. 'What an accursed thing homelessness is!', John Steinbeck echoes in *The Grapes of Wrath* (#1 novel in 1939). 'What an accursed thing anti-Semitism is', echoes Laura Z. Hobson in *Gentleman's Agreement* (#1 novel in 1947; 'a banned book, a number one title, and an underappreciated minor modernist masterpiece', as John Unsworth describes it). Stowe's righteous curse rings recurrently through her country's bestseller lists.

Whether or not Stowe caused it, during the American Civil War itself, the most popular reading matter among combatants on both sides were pirated copies of *Les Misérables*. The story of the galley slave Jean Valjean is probably the most bloodstained novel in the history of literature. Miserable indeed. Victor Hugo received not a sou, as he pulled away at his literary oar.

It was noteworthy that Stowe was a woman: women's mark was heavier on mid-century American popular fiction than on its British counterpart. This was particularly evident in the so-called 'feminized fifties', a decade dominated by such works as Miss Maria S. Cummins's *The Lamplighter* (a recycling of George Eliot's *Silas Marner*) and Mary Jane Holmes's *Tempest and Sunshine* (1854). Written by women, for women, about women's interests and problems, such novels indicated a distinct difference from British patterns of readership and what George Eliot called 'silly novels by lady novelists'. As in abolitionism, women were a powerful lobby in American book culture.

Eight years after *Uncle Tom's Cabin*, yet another woman, Ann S. Stephens, is credited with authorship of the first 'dime novel', *Malaeska, the Indian Wife of the White Hunter* (1860). Among other bestselling, and much imitated, dime novels were the 'Deadwood Dick' and 'Buffalo Bill Cody' series, by many (predominantly male) hands.

As the titles indicate, these 10c productions were proto-westerns. Dime novels were also, two decades later, the launch pad for proto-detective fiction, with the 'Nick Carter' series. The young 'tec survived in pulps, radio serials, comic books, and films until the 1920s – still a juvenile crime-buster at an age when celebratory telegrams from J. Edgar Hoover would have been in order.

Nick Carter was another multi-hand creation, although one hand in particular, that of Frederic van Rensselaer Dey, claims authorship of a thousand or more 'Carters' – typically portraying the hero in mortal combat with the perversely immortal series villain, Doc Quartz.

Women are elsewhere prominent in the genesis era of American bestsellerdom. A conventional starting point for the American detective novel proper is Anna Katherine Green's *The Leavenworth Case* (1878), a whodunit that introduced the immensely loved series hero, Ebenezer Gryce – a sleuth as quirky as his name. The detective genre was quickly colonized by male writers.

By the 1870s, American popular fiction had developed a remarkable speed of response to current events – as witnessed by E. P. Roe's religious romance set against the great Chicago fire of 1871, *Barriers Burned Away*. Newspapers would regularly supply material for opportunistic writers of popular fiction over the next century, bouncing headline events between them.

The pulp link between newspaper and novel had been established as early as 1840, with what is called the 'Great Revolution' in American bookselling: namely, the distribution in the 1840s of novels as 'extras', supplements given away with newspapers. The innovation is credited to two New York journalists, Park Benjamin and Rufus Wilmot Griswold.

There were other than newspaper-reading constituencies to cater for: congregations, notably. Ever since its foundation, America has been as much a Bible- as a novel-reading nation. Lew Wallace's *Ben Hur: A Tale of the Christ* (1880) was that useful thing – a novel that could be read on Sunday (unfurtively).

Massively long (Harper priced it at a deterrent $1.50) and densely researched (the author gave up his law practice to write it), Wallace's epic story of Ben Hur – Prince of Judea, galley slave, chariot jockey, and, finally, Christian disciple – was slow to take off. But, boosted by Sunday-school commendation, sales had reached the million mark when in 1913, Harper's sold a further one million copies, at one go, to the department store Sears, Roebuck – the biggest ever single order for a work of fiction. The spectacular film version of 1925, starring Ramon Novarro, led to another boom in *Ben Hur*'s sales, as did the Charlton Heston (Gore Vidal-scripted) 1959 movie.

On the fringe of the religious market for fiction were such essentially improving works for the younger reader as Louisa May Alcott's *Little Women* (1868). And, more preachingly, the rags-to-riches homilies of Horatio Alger. A Unitarian minister, Alger infused evangelical fervour into such social-Darwinistic tracts as *Ragged Dick, or Street Life in New York with the Boot Blacks* (1868) and *Mark the Match Boy* (1869) and sold strongly for half a century. The genre is deliciously, and bitterly, satirized by Nathanael West in *A Cool Million* (1934) and more affectionately in the film *Forrest Gump*. Alger remains deeply embedded in the American soul, as an ideal and an irritant.

When he declared that 'all' American literature began with *Huckleberry Finn* (1885), Ernest Hemingway meant that Twain had forged a distinctly national idiom and voice. One can, however, point to an earlier generation of popular novels, appealing to mass readerships through their comic use of regional dialects, such as the 'Hoosier tales' of Edward Eggleston. These anti-pastorals, with their authentically registered Indiana speech, enjoyed huge success, notably *The Hoosier Schoolmaster* (1871). A parallel success in Britain was enjoyed by the 'Kailyard' (cabbage patch – Scottish cabbage, that is) school – notably Ian Maclaren's and J. M. Barrie's sentimentalized depictions of life in 'Drumtochty' and 'Thrums' (i.e. 'loose threads').

The Hoosier novels were targeted at family and younger readers. Distinctly adult in his appeal, Émile Zola had an easier ride into American popular culture than in England, where his luckless publisher, Henry Vizetelly, was imprisoned for throwing, as the authorities put it, a vial of acid in the face of the British reading public. Zola was conceived to be well beyond the traditional blush on the maiden's cheek. Works such as *Nana* (1880) sold powerfully in translation in America (if less well than Hugo) and home-grown Zolaism took off with Stephen Crane's *Maggie, a Girl of the Streets* (1893), notably more explicit than its British Zolaesque counterpart, George Moore's *Esther Waters* (1894). American 'naturalism' would reach its apogee with Upton Sinclair's *j'accuse* against the Chicago stockyards, *The Jungle* (#6, 1906) – a novel so scathing in its 'muckraking' that the president, Theodore Roosevelt, dispatched a commission of inquiry to the city, to verify whether the 'fiction' was 'fact'. It was, they reported.

The arrival of the lists, 1895–1910

Logically enough, it was in America that the first bestseller lists originated. *The Adventures of Captain Horn*, by Frank R. Stockton, claims the title of the first #1 *listed* bestseller in literary history. A rollicking 'gold fever' yarn, it coincided, excitingly, with contemporary gold-rushes to Alaska (a future bestselling author, Jack London, was actually hacking into the snowy wastes at the time; he would eventually strike it richer with bestselling fiction).

Stockton is one of the forgottens of literary history. Equally forgotten is the novelist reputed to have been the first not merely to have sold millions, but to have made millions. Harold Bell Wright (1872–1944) was a Baptist minister whose first bestseller (of 18), *That Printer of Udell's*, was initially designed to be read aloud to his Ozark congregation. 'Plain food for plain people', Wright called his improving fiction. That plainest of presidents, Ronald Reagan, credited *That Printer of Udell's* as having changed his life, 'in my growing-up years... After reading it and thinking about it for a few days, I went to my mother and told her I wanted to be baptized'. Thus was the foe of the Evil Empire set on his path of righteousness.

The 20th century opened with what was plausibly claimed to be the (then) fastest-selling novel of all time, Irving Bacheller's *Eben Holden* (1900). It was, appropriately enough for the period, as millions poured through Ellis Island, a romance of immigration. Bacheller's novel was propelled by dynamic advertising, as the 20th century's accelerated tempo was reflected in a market ravenous for fast, aggressively 'pushed' fiction.

The appetite for fast-fictional-food found a successful exponent in O. Henry (William Sydney Porter), 'The Yankee Maupassant'. The man behind the *nom de plume* had begun writing his short, smart stories while a prisoner, on charges of embezzlement, in 1901 – a rags to riches career that not even Alger could have improved upon.

War, pulp, and movies

As important as any single bestseller was the emergence of genre – particularly in its ultra-cheap 'pulp' form. F. A. Munsey's 10c *All Story Magazine* achieved a circulation of half a million by 1907, and helped launch the careers of Zane Grey, Edgar Rice Burroughs, and Max Brand, and with them a mass demand for the 'western' (e.g. *Riders of the Purple Sage*), fantasy (*Tarzan of the Apes*), and crime (Nick Carter, inevitably). Pulp formed a mutually beneficial alliance with celluloid. The motion picture had become a marketable commodity with the *Great Train Robbery* (a dime novel narrative) in 1903. The first novel to be 'optioned' was Thomas Dixon's odious paean to the Ku Klux Klan, *The Clansman* (1905), for whose subsidiary rights D. W. Griffiths paid $2,000. The result was *The Birth of a Nation* (1915) – for many years the top-grossing film in America.

Rex Beach ('the poor man's Jack London') regularly led the *Bookman* lists in the early years of the century with his manly tales of the Yukon gold strikes which began with *Pardners* (1905). Shrewdly, Beach set up his own film company to exploit his property. So, as it happened, did Jack London. The 'tie-in' was born.

As John G. Cawelti has argued, 'melodrama' is a main (arguably *the* main) strand in American popular fiction through the decades. The panoramic, broad-canvas 'melo' was exploited, with spectacular success, by Winston Churchill (the other one), whose popularity peaked with *A High Country* (#1, 1915), the story of an American prodigal son, Hugh Paret, from error-strewn boyhood to manly maturity.

Churchill's bestselling formula can be traced down to such later exponents of the high (and bestselling) melodramatic style as James T. Farrell, John O'Hara, and Herman Wouk. The Great American Novel may have proved elusive; the Big American Bestseller less so.

Less ambitiously than Churchill, Booth Tarkington popularized the trials of adolescence (a category of life invented in America at this period by G. Stanley Hall) in wryly amused bestsellers such as *Penrod* (1914) and *Seventeen* (1916). The young reader had always been more of a force in (more literate) America than in Europe, and with 18-year-olds dying by the hundred thousand in France in 1914–18, Tarkington's idylls enjoyed an added escapist charm (his most enduring work, thanks to Orson Welles, is another study of adolescent agonistes, *The Magnificent Ambersons*).

The Great War precipitated a palpable surge of Anglophilia in the American bestselling lists. For example, 1917 (the year the US entered the conflict) saw H. G. Wells's novel of patriotic-parental bereavement, *Mr Britling Sees It Through*, at the top of the American list ('Britling' = 'Little Brit'). Wells was, other than in these unusual times, very much an exclusive Little Brit taste.

The special relationship in fiction peaked in the '*annus mirabilis*' (discussed in Chapter 1). Beaux legionnaires, Jeevesian gentlemen's gentlemen, blue lagoons, and deliciously ravaging sheiks dominated page and screen: all invented by good English ink. The rage for things English also sucked in works of (arguably) high literary quality such as Michael Arlen's cosmopolitan comedy, *The Green Hat* (1925), with its daring 'syphilis' theme, and, in the same year, Margaret Kennedy's *The Constant Nymph*, whose 15-year-old, sexually active heroine eerily prefigures Vladimir Nabokov's 1957 bestseller about a less constant nymph(et), *Lolita*. Warwick Deeping's *Sorrell and Son* was hugely to the American taste, as had been A. S. M. Hutchinson's 1921 novel on the same, ex-officer-unrewarded theme, *If Winter Comes* (#1 novel in the US in 1922).

Rarely, since 1895, had British taste so converged with the American bestseller. The English incursion continued, less dominatingly, over the following decade with works such as James Hilton's Shangri-La romance *Lost Horizon* (#5, 1935) and *Goodbye Mr Chips* (#4, 1934). What Americans in the heartland made of the retirement of an English public schoolmaster can only be imagined. Tibet probably seemed more familiar.

At the end of the decade, a growing anti-militarism manifested itself with *All Quiet on the Western Front* (#1, 1929), the only German novel to have won the #1 accolade. It corresponded with a mood of anti-war isolationism in the US and was, in popular fiction terms, the equivalent of students at Oxford University voting not to die for King and Country. A collective 'No!' to war; or, perhaps, given what was happening on the streets of Germany, a 'No, *not again*!'

American national themes still sold strongly. Edna Ferber inaugurated what would be a string of chauvinist epics with *So Big* (#1, 1925). Ferber's overwhelmingly popular and even more overwhelmingly massive novels included *Show Boat* (1926), which was adapted into a musical by Jerome Kern and Oscar Hammerstein that has lasted rather better than the source text. So too *Cimarron* (#1, 1930), a tale of the Oklahoma land rush. Ferber's career in bestsellers concluded some three decades later with *Giant* (1952), the dynastic saga of two generations of Texan oil magnates, which was filmed in 1956, starring James Dean and Elizabeth Taylor. In fact, Ferber's 12 novels and 9 plays were furnished into 20 appropriately 'big' films – a record. John Unsworth notes:

> I think she may have the honour of having the longest run on the bestseller list, in terms of the span of years, in the 20th century. She also has the honour of coming from the same town that produced Harry Houdini and Joe McCarthy (Appleton, Wisconsin), and possibly of being the first nearly openly lesbian bestselling author. Ferber is a gold-mine.

The 1920s witnessed a distinguished convergence of literary quality and mass popularity with the #1 title of 1927, Thornton Wilder's *The Bridge of San Luis Rey*. The narrative opens with a (historical) bridge collapse in Peru on 20 July 1714 and goes on to reconstruct, deftly and intertwiningly, the (fictional) lives of the five travellers killed in the disaster.

Wilder headed the lists again, ten years later, with *Heaven's My Destination*, a Voltairean satire on Sinclair Lewis's blast against the 'religion business' (predatory, donation-sucking evangelism) *Elmer Gantry*. Lewis's clumpingly un-Voltairean novel was itself a #1 title, selling 200,000 copies in its first week of publication in 1927.

One of the more interesting subgenres of popular fiction in the 1920s was the so-called 'sex novel' – typically a light confection combining raciness, urban sophistication, and jazz-age flapperdom. The best, and most enduring, of these works was Anita Loos's *Gentlemen Prefer Blondes* (#1, 1926). Adapted from a *New Yorker* serial, written in deliciously comic semi-literate style, Loos's novel pioneered a gallery of enduring sexual stereotypes. The work was filmed (starring, inevitably, Marilyn Monroe) in 1953. Loos's book also has the distinction of being one of the last illustrated bestsellers for grown-ups until the late 20th-century 'graphic novel'.

Gentlemen Prefer Blondes shared top place in the 1926 lists with the equally deft comic fantasia, *The Private Life of Helen of Troy* by John Erskine – flapperdom Trojan-style. Other, less noteworthy, sex novels of the period are Vina Delmar's *Bad Girl* (1928), the story of Dot Haley, a loose-moralled telephone operator, and Donald Henderson's *Impatient Virgin* (1931) – the titles say it all.

These self-consciously 'daring' novels signalled a widening of the aperture of permissibility – something bulldozed through in Erskine Caldwell's steamy sex and Southern squalor tales, *God's Little Acre* (1933) and *Tobacco Road* (1932).

Genre: romance, the western, crime, science fiction, horror

Caldwell's bestsellers were notable not merely for their explicitness, but for his publishing them 'new', in 25c paperback form. They were marketed, that is, as if they were genre products – prole-fic.

Five main categories of genre fiction came to the fore in the 20th century. The most venerable is romance, following a direct line from Susanna Haswell to Danielle Steel, from the Minerva Press to Mills & Boon, and catering mainly for the female reader. The primal male action genre – rooted in the dime novel – is the western, or cowboy romance. Owen Wister, author of *The Virginian: A Horseman of the Plains* (#1, 1902), declared the American West to be 'the great playground of young men' (Wister, like many other 'lungers' of the period, went West not to play, but for his pulmonary health).

It would be a favourite location for male readers of all ages. Wister it was who supplied the formula for Zane Grey's 200 or so westerns, of which the most famous (so famous that they actually made the top ten bestseller lists in their year of publication) were *Riders of the Purple Sage* (1912) and *The Lone Star Ranger* (1915). At his heyday, Grey could plausibly claim to be the most popular author in the English-speaking world. Lifetime sales of his novels (boosted by over 100 film adaptations) are estimated at 250 million and still growing. Following the trail he blazed was Clarence E. Mulford with his Bar-20 cowpoke, Hopalong Cassidy, introduced in 1912 and played, heroically, by William Boyd on screen for 20 years, at the end of which it was more Crawlalong than Hop.

Street and Smith's *Western Story Magazine*, begun in 1919, and costing a talismanic dime, launched the career of Max Brand, who finally checked in his 'red-hot typewriter' (as he called it) with the undisputed title, in the 1930s, of 'King of the Pulps'. From 1917 until his death in 1944, Brand poured out an estimated 30 million words of fiction, some 900 stories and around 600 full-length novels, under as many as 20 pen names, and in all the major popular fiction genres (westerns, mysteries, hospital stories, melodramas, even science fiction). Brand's formula was simplicity itself: 'All you have to do is concentrate on a snappy beginning and a smash for the close.' Brand's first novel was *The Untamed* (1919), and his most famous, *Destry Rides Again* (1930), was filmed with Marlene Dietrich.

Brand's crown passed on to Louis L'Amour, whose first big hit, *Hondo* (1952), was boosted by a John Wayne movie. 'Best Western I've ever read', declared Wayne, who bought the rights. Always a favourite with the right wing, L'Amour was awarded a Congressional Medal of Honor by Ronald Reagan, who regretted that, unlike the Duke, he had never starred in a L'Amour movie. Unlike Brand (a lifelong city slicker), L'Amour actually lived in the West. He has some 200 titles to his credit, and claimed worldwide sales of over 225 million.

Other distinguished performers in the genre include Ernest Haycox, whose *Stage Coach to Lordsburg* (1938) was adapted into the classic John Ford film *Stage Coach* (1939), with John Wayne as the Ringo Kid. Of all the genres, the western was the most directly boosted by cinema.

The third of the venerable genres is the crime-based detective story. The early decades of the 20th century are seen as the golden age of this genre. S. S. van Dine's patrician sleuth Philo Vance (Lord Peter Wimsey's American cousin) is one of myriad popular series heroes. It was van Dine who introduced the famous 'twenty rules' for golden-age detective fiction (the principal of which was flagrantly, famously, and artfully broken by Agatha Christie's *The Murder of Roger Ackroyd*).

The Anglophile or, as Orwell called it, the 'Raffles' taint was scoured away with the launch of the *Black Mask* magazine in 1926, whose editor, Captain Joseph T. Shaw, pioneered the 'hard-boiled' crime, detection, and private eye thrillers of Dashiell Hammett. Hammett's *The Maltese Falcon*, in 1930, introduced the archetypal Sam Spade. Shaw also published James M. Cain's *noir* masterpiece *The Postman Always Rings Twice* (1934) and Raymond Chandler, whose Philip Marlowe ('son of Spade') was introduced in 1938 with *The Big Sleep*. The softer-boiled variety of detective story continued with Rex Stout's Nero Wolfe and his Watson, Archie Goodwin, along with many others.

As with westerns, the productivity of the leaders in the genre was legendary. Harry Bedford Jones was, in the 1930s, selling by the million under some ten pseudonyms. Jones graciously ceded his title 'King of the Woodpulps' to Erle Stanley Gardner in March 1933 on receiving a complimentary copy of the first Perry Mason adventure, *The Case of the Velvet Claws*.

Gardner, under *his* battery of pen names, would sell over 300 million copies of his crime and mystery novels over the next four decades. His most famous creation, the infallible criminal defence lawyer Perry Mason, was given an extra lease of life by the television series, broadcast 1957–66. As a crime writer, Gardner was, when he finally laid down his pen, kinging it as much over the Tube as the Woodpulps.

Science fiction (with its allied subgenres, fantasy, horror, and gothic) is the fourth of the great pulp families. The patriarchal figure in this period is Edgar Rice Burroughs. Burroughs, as a young man, had steeped himself in Darwin. It inspired his most famous conception, *Tarzan of the Apes*, introduced in 1912, swinging and yodelling with his simian ancestors through the jungle. The year before, in *Munsey's All Story Magazine*, Burroughs had launched his equally popular *John Carter of Mars* series. His hollow-earth *Pellucidar* series was begun in 1914. With these bestselling franchises in his stable, the author incorporated himself as 'Edgar Rice Burroughs Inc.' in 1923. He was earning the then fabulous sum of $100,000 per year. Burroughs would go on to publish some 70 novels, and can claim to be the Henry Ford of genre fiction – its most efficient mass producer for the mass market.

A purer form of science fiction was distilled in Hugo Gernsback's magazine *Amazing Stories*, founded in 1926. Gernsback redefined the genre in terms of the equation: 'Science + Fiction = SF'. After being taken over by John W. Campbell in 1937, *Amazing Stories* became the nursery for such new talents in the genre as Isaac

Asimov, Robert Heinlein, and Theodore Sturgeon. Campbell used his editorship to push a hard-right political view – reflected in the work of Heinlein especially long after he left the *Amazing Stories* fold. Heinlein's motto, 'TANSTAAFL' ('there ain't no such thing as a free lunch'), proclaimed in *The Moon is a Harsh Mistress* (1966), has migrated from fiction into American political discourse.

The huge market opened up by the genre/pulp fiction factories was looked at, both enviously and disdainfully, by the 'literary' sector. William Faulkner (later a Nobellist) composed *Sanctuary* (1931) by asking himself what would sell 10,000 copies, then 'invented the most horrific tale I could imagine and wrote it in about three weeks'. The tale of sadistic rape and violence duly sold its expected quantity. Less cynically, Ernest Hemingway (another future Nobellist) absorbed an idiom strikingly like that of the 'hard-boiled' crime writers into his fiction.

John Unsworth would add to this popular fiction cluster the 'mob novel', which he sees as a genre 'separate from the crime novel, importantly displacing the western. In the western, starting with *The Virginian*, the prototypical plot favors the law over the outlaw (exceptions prove the rule); in the mob novel, the reverse is true.' As he further notes, the mob novel, which reaches its mature form in Mario Puzo's *The Godfather*, 'pretty much kills off the western in movies and TV, right through to *The Sopranos*'.

Blockbusterism

As genre diversified its energies through a plethora of titles and styles, so, elsewhere, popular fiction concentrated its formidable force into the single 'blockbuster' (the image is taken from dynamiting).

It was largely a function of the growing importance of the bestseller list in the US and increasing efficiency of delivery systems (including, massively, book clubs) and film-magazine-book tie-in. One can conveniently mark the arrival of this blockbusting ware with Hervey Allen's *Anthony Adverse* (#1, 1933). At 1,200 pages, and costing a whopping $3, the publishers, Farrar and Rinehart, advertised Allen's 18th-century tale of buccaneering and adventure on the high seas as 'three books for the price of one' and 'the longest novel ever published': it was both block and blockbuster.

Boosted as a Book of the Month Club title and by an Oscar-winning 1936 film adaptation, *Anthony Adverse* topped the American bestseller list for two years. A notable innovation was the novel's sexual explicitness, with scenes set in brothels and direct reference to 'erections' and 'orgasms' (an aspect of the novel prudently excised for the mass movie audience). This was costume drama for adults; Rafael Sabatini plus sex – a new and exciting mixture for the popular palate.

The success of Allen's novel (which he never contrived to repeat) created new parameters of bestsellerism. None the less, the main line of top-selling titles through the 1930s remained that traditional mainstay of the lists: melodrama. Pearl S. Buck's saga of the self-improving Chinese coolie Wang Lung, *The Good Earth* (#1, 1931), earned her a fortune at the beginning of the decade and a Nobel Prize at its end, in 1938 (sympathy engendered by the Japanese invasion of China helped).

An offshoot of melodrama, the 'doctor's tale', caught the public fancy in 1935, with Lloyd C. Douglas's *The Green Light* (#1, 1935), a 'surgeon's dilemma' narrative. This line of 'white coat + stethoscope' fiction was developed into an inexhaustibly popular genre in 1940 with the versatile Max Brand's *Calling Dr Kildare* – the first of a series of formulaic hospital dramas chronicling the trials of a young Irish American physician, his wise old mentor, Dr Leonard Gillespie, and the love of his life, nurse Mary Lamont. Kildare was absorbed into the emergent television medium and was the procreator of such subsequent 'soaps' (on the small screen and in novelization) as *Marcus Welby*, *M*A*S*H*, and *E.R.*

Not all doctors in popular fiction were saintly. Ambivalence about the knife-wielding profession was given memorable expression in Henry Bellamann's bestselling title of 1940, *King's Row*, in which the villainous Dr Gordon amputates the legs of a young man he considers ineligible as a suitor for his daughter. The novel was filmed in 1942, with Ronald Reagan as the luckless, limbless Drake McHugh, delivering his most famous line (on coming round from the operation), 'Where's the rest of me?'

The depiction of the unrelenting malignity of small-town life in *King's Row*, drawing on Sinclair Lewis's *Main Street* (#1, 1921) and *Babbitt* (#4, 1923), anticipates Grace Metalious's 1957 superseller *Peyton Place*. Bestsellers over the century register, more sensitively than the sociologists, the tensions between metropolitan, rural, and suburban America: a line that can be traced down to John Updike's *Couples* (#2, 1968) and, for the curious mind, Stephen King's *It* (#1, 1986).

Rarely have the poles of realism and romance been more divided than in the bestsellers of the late 1930s. Daphne du Maurier's *Rebecca* (#4, 1938) – the most skilful of many updatings of *Jane Eyre* – was notable not merely as an archetypally English novel triumphing in America, but for achieving a durable success by virtue of Alfred Hitchcock's (archetypally English) Hollywood version in 1940.

Margaret Mitchell's hyper-romantic *Gone with the Wind* (#1, 1936) out-blockbustered even *Anthony Adverse*, with sales of a million in its first year. Its American Civil War canvas was vast and panoramic and, with Europe descending into chaos and the scars of the Great Depression unhealed, deeply escapist.

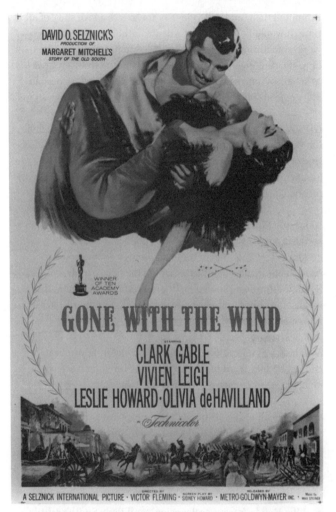

7. *Gone with the Wind*: 'the greatest love story of all time' in full technicolour

Promoted then (and still today) as 'the greatest love story of all time', it would be the reticent Atlanta author's only published work, something that has always added to its mystique. The 1939 film, starring Vivien Leigh and Clark Gable, tactfully omitted Mitchell's admiring depictions of the Ku Klux Klan, as perhaps 'the greatest (racist) love story' would not have gone down so well.

GWTW (as devotees call it) enjoyed a second lease of bestselling life with the estate-authorized *Scarlett*, which was the top-selling title of 1991. Alexandra Ripley's sequel takes off from the 'tomorrow is another day' line with which Mitchell open-endedly finished her novel.

Alongside Mitchell's historical melodrama, John Steinbeck's social-protest tract *The Grapes of Wrath* headed the 1939 bestseller list. The story of the Joad family's doomed odyssey from their parched Oklahoma farm to the false paradise of South California promoted, with propagandistic urgency, the idealisms of Roosevelt's New Deal, crossed with the author's own idiosyncratic neo-Darwinism.

Steinbeck's novel was filmed, with a disconcertingly upbeat ending, by John Ford in 1940. The Joads' lurching truck was a planet away from Tara or Manderley.

World War II, as had its predecessor, propelled British authors such as A. J. Cronin and Richard Llewellyn to the top of the American bestseller list. The war also darkened the environment. The line of social seriousness introduced by Steinbeck was continued with such #1 bestsellers as Lillian Smith's anti-lynching polemic *Strange Fruit* (#1, 1944; subsequently immortalized by Billie Holiday's jazz vocal version), and Betty Smith's grittily sub-Dreiser *A Tree Grows in Brooklyn* (#4, 1943).

Also continued was the line of *Anthony Adverse*-style blockbusting romance – most successfully with Kathleen Winsor's English

8. *The Grapes of Wrath* (1939), first edition

Civil War romp *Forever Amber* (#4, 1944). The enterprising heroine, Amber St Clare, sleeps with everyone, including the merry monarch himself. Her motto is 'adultery's no crime – it's an amusement'. The novel profited immensely from its 'banned in Boston' outrageousness.

A rather milder costume drama (but none the less highly salesworthy) was popularized by Frank Yerby, with his antebellum (Civil War, that is) romance *The Foxes of Harrow* (1946). Yerby is notable as the first African American to have made the bestseller lists. His, however, is not a name advanced with much pride by historians of black American culture. It was not until 1969, well after the 1964 Civil Rights Act (and James Baldwin's emergence as a widely admired writer), that Yerby's romance featured an African American protagonist.

Postwar

In 1946, Robert Penn Warren (one of the most eminent critics of his time, and a theorist of the Faulknerian 'Southern School' of fiction) produced what was, probably, the best 'literary' #1 bestseller of the immediate postwar period, *All the King's Men*, a *roman-à-clef* based on the Louisiana demagogue Huey Long. The World War had, it seemed, made America more thoughtful about the ideals its citizens were fighting for.

National conscience was wrenched even more violently by Laura Z. Hobson's exposure of the discreet mechanisms of anti-Semitism in *Gentleman's Agreement* (#1, 1947), filmed the same year, starring Gregory Peck as the journalist Philip Green, who pretends to be Jewish to experience prejudice first hand. The solemnly well-meaning film won three Oscars. But it suggested – with the mass elevation of public education engendered by the postwar GI Bill – that the American bestseller was decades ahead of the American political establishment in terms of civil rights, and could act as an agent of social enlightenment. *Could* but, in the event, did not. Unhappily, the McCarthyite purge, at the end of the decade, neutered the medium for decades.

There was, oddly, no serious bestseller about World War II, from the serving soldier's point of view, until Norman Mailer's *The Naked and the Dead* (#2, 1948). The ex-rifleman author introduced barrack-room explicitness into American popular fiction – specifically with the profuse scattering throughout his text of the 'three-letter word', 'fug'. It elicited the notable greeting from Dorothy Parker: 'so *you're* the young man who can't spell fuck.'

Mailer opened a floodgate. In 1951, James Jones's *From Here to Eternity* was the year's #1 bestseller, and Herman Wouk's *The Caine Mutiny* was #2. These novels aimed, as Jones put it, 'to blow the lid off the war'; fugging war, he might have said.

A more ponderous approach to great issues was evident in the saga of the Apostle Peter, *The Big Fisherman*, by Lloyd C. Douglas, which topped bestseller lists in 1948. Douglas had been a Lutheran minister before becoming a popular novelist and, like Wright and Wallace before him, used bestselling fiction as a God given pulpit for his new congregation of millions. The creation of the state of Israel gave a collateral lift to his popularity. Douglas's 1942 bestseller, about the most sacred relic of the crucifixion, *The Robe*, was filmed in the grand Cecil B. DeMille technicolor style in 1953. The film propelled the somewhat antiquated novel into the #1 slot that year, for a second time.

Crime fiction was, in the mid-1940s, even harder-boiled than it had been in trend-setting *Black Mask* days. The depths of human depravity revealed by the liberation of Germany and the ruthlessness of the War in the Pacific were reflected in the genre. W. R. Burnett's *The Asphalt Jungle* (1949) opened with a quotation from William James: 'man is the most formidable of all beasts of prey, and indeed the only one that preys systematically on his own species.'

The most predatory invention was Mickey Spillane's series hero, Mike Hammer, introduced in *I, the Jury* (1947). The vigilante private eye (former marine) played executioner as well as jury, on the last page, by shooting a woman in the stomach. 'It was easy', Hammer observes laconically, after carrying out his personally adjudicated death sentence. For several years, Spillane's paperback sales of Hammer novels (which, if pushed, he could turn out in three days apiece) outstripped all rivals in the US. The taste for his work was widely deplored – gorilla-fiction, Raymond Chandler called it – 'people like them', Spillane blandly responded. Indeed they did: he outsold all rivals year in, year out.

The 1950s

There was, in the Eisenhower era, an equally voracious taste for meaty, above all 'filmable', novels which dealt, ponderously, with moral dilemmas and 'big' issues. Henry Morton Robinson made it to the top of the 1950 bestseller list with his life-and-trials (sexual, mainly) story of an American prince of the Catholic Church, *The Cardinal*. He followed up with the #1 title of 1954, *Not as a Stranger*. This multi-stranded story of young men undergoing medical training would be much imitated – not least in television soap operas (soap and white coats being natural partners).

As had Edward Bellamy's *Looking Backward* in the 1880s, Ayn Rand's paean to capitalism, *Atlas Shrugged*, popularized the author's 'objectivist philosophy', more frankly summed up as the 'doctrine of the dollar'. In the novel, a union of big businessmen – 'wealth creators' – resolve to 'go on strike'. Society collapses, proving that the world needs capitalism: the rich are always with you.

A slow starter (it made only #10 on the 1957 list – eight places behind *Peyton Place*), Rand's massive tract had sold five million copies (and made her many doctrinal dollars) by 1984, and had influenced many of America's key decision makers – including, momentously, Alan Greenspan. No novel, since *Uncle Tom's Cabin*, has been as politically influential.

Rand was one of the three 'Russians' to figure on the bestseller lists in the late 1960s. Vladimir Nabokov's paedophile fantasia, *Lolita*, was, after some years' nervous suppression and underground circulation in Paris, released in the US in 1959. It shot to the top of the bestseller lists, to be challenged, over succeeding months, by Boris Pasternak's *Doctor Zhivago* – a work that could only be read in samizdat version in the author's native USSR. Nabokov became rich, while Pasternak was offered a consolatory Nobel Prize (which the Soviet authorities forbade him from accepting). Pasternak's seditious narrative of the Revolution 'from below' is unique in having the CIA's publicity department help it to its overwhelming sales success in the West.

The 1960s

The early 1960s bestseller lists were dominated by Irving Stone's massive biographical novels, or 'biofictions', such as *The Agony and the Ecstasy* (#1, 1961), based on the life of Michelangelo and requiring, the author recorded, six years' research – a doctorate's worth. It was made into a suitably reverent film, starring Charlton Heston.

Stone's massiveness of biofictional design was rivalled by the geofictions of James T. Michener, whose first epic, *Hawaii*, topped the American lists in 1959, coinciding with the Pacific islands' accession to statehood. As his acknowledgement pages record, Michener was aided by teams of researchers. By 1983, he had run out of terrestrial sites and had the #2 bestseller of the year with *Space*. Ever since Fenimore Cooper sent a geriatric Natty Bumpo out West (in *The Prairie*, 1827), there had always been new frontiers for American writers to traverse, demarcate, and celebrate.

From a book trade point of view, the most significant work of popular fiction over the year 1959–60 was a 30-year-old romance of illicit love in the English woods by a long-dead author – D. H. Lawrence's *Lady Chatterley's Lover*. The novel had long been banned, for its 'four-letter words' and sexual 'bouts'. The times had changed, and Lawrence's antique *roman à thèse* was cleared for publication in successive court hearings and – not being protected under American copyright law – duly pirated with a zest not seen since the good old days of the 1880s. The avalanche of cheap reprints of *Lady Chatterley's Lover* unloaded on the American public is plausibly credited with triggering the 1960s 'paperback revolution'.

Post-Lawrentian 'permissiveness' made possible not only literary efforts like Philip Roth's celebration of heroically Semitic onanism, *Portnoy's Complaint* (#1, 1969), but a new fictional brutalism most emetically displayed in Harold Robbins's series of supersellers beginning with *The Carpetbaggers* (#5, 1961 – massively more popular in paperback), a biofiction of the eccentric aviator and film producer Howard Hughes, superheated with graphic sex and even more graphic sadism. It features, for example, a scene in which the hero identifies the man who tortured and killed his mother by the tobacco pouch which he has made from the luckless woman's breast. Lawrence would have been appalled.

For the consumer of less salacious wares, Arthur Hailey began his series of densely researched novels with *Hotel* (#1, 1965), an updating of Vicki Baum's earlier bestselling *Grand Hotel* (1931). The English-born, but thoroughly Americanized, author would go on to cover airports, banks, car factories, hospitals, and power stations. It took him, Hailey claimed, four years to produce a novel: three years' research, one year's writing. Hailey had throughout the late 1960s and 1970s a golden touch as he instructed Americans about how modern America worked.

Genre fiction had, since World War II, progressed well beyond its pulpy origins and aspired – at its top levels – to high literary respectability. Much of the credit was due to the self-adjudicating nature of these lines of 'category' fiction through their institutional awards, such as Edgars (after the father of detective fiction, Edgar Allan Poe), or Hugos (after the father of science fiction, Hugo Gernsback). French intellectual reverence for *noir* (Hammett, Chester Himes, Jim Thompson, and others) added another layer of dark dignity.

In addition to its ever popular (Ellery Queen) staples, genre had diversified in unconventional ways. Himes, with the first of his Coffin Ed Johnson and Gravedigger Jones cop stories, *A Rage in Harlem* (1967), successfully mixed Frantz Fanon *noir* and African American negritude. Tony Hillerman introduced an even more unusual line of *romans policiers* with his Navajo cops, Joe Leaphorn and Jim Chee, in *The Blessing Way* (1970). The most critically admired writer in the crime-adventure genre, Elmore Leonard, gave up writing film scripts and embarked on a new and fabulously successful career with *The Big Bounce* in 1969.

Science fiction was similarly raising itself (to the distress of its harder-line fans). Ray Bradbury, with novels such as *Fahrenheit 451* (1953), his satire on the new television-driven philistinism, broke out of the science fiction ghetto into mass readership and high critical respect. He was, cynics said, the favourite science fiction writer for readers who did not like science fiction (or television). Epics such as Frank Herbert's *Dune* (1965), which had originated with research into the preservation of Oregon's coastline, became cult classics, as did Isaac Asimov's *Foundation* trilogy (1951). They were even studied on American campuses – that deadliest of accolades.

Women's romance entered new uninhibited territory with Jacqueline Susann's *The Valley of the Dolls* (#1, 1966; for some years entered in *The Guinness Book of Records* as the all-time bestselling work of fiction). The narrative follows the intertwined stories of three pill (i.e. 'doll') popping young sexual adventurers ('dolls' of the other kind) in New York. Susann's novel – promoted by her own highly marketable fashion model image – blazed a trail for what later became known as bodice-rippers: 'women's romance without the iron knickers' as the irreverent British practitioner, Molly Parkin, called them.

The mood of the late 1960s, even in straight melodrama, was notably dissident. Everything was ripping, not just bodices. Even the American Dream. Elia Kazan's *The Arrangement* (#1, 1967) is the portrait of an individual who had been called, after Sloan Wilson's 1955 bestseller, 'a man in a gray flannel suit'. Kazan's man in a gray flannel suit is a cigarette advertising executive who methodically destroys the successful life he has laboriously constructed for himself, as the Surgeon General's devastating 1964 report on smoking and cancer darkens the background.

Pro-Vietnam War novels such as Robin Moore's *The Green Berets* (#5, 1965) attracted obloquy in equal measure to their success, reflecting a bitterly divided nation. Moore's novel was filmed by John Wayne, starring John Wayne winning the war his America lost.

There remained some things America could agree on. Michael Crichton's technothriller *The Andromeda Strain* (#5, 1969) was the first 'true' science fiction novel to make it into the upper reaches of the annual bestseller lists. A celebration of American (specifically NASA's) science, it was boosted by the chauvinist publicity for the Apollo moon landings. The Vietcong may not have been beaten, but the USSR was thoroughly outrun in the two-horse race for the moon which President Kennedy had announced in 1963. Arthur C. Clarke's 1968 'novelization' of Stanley Kubrick's film *2001* (itself based on one of the English science fiction writer's short stories) also hitch-hiked to success on Apollo. Clarke hit the lists over following years with decennial sequels from *2010* to *2060*. All were suffused with the cosmic optimism he derived from his master in the science-fiction-utopian genre, Olaf Stapledon.

The late 1960s and 1970s are notable for new scales of sale – in both hard- and paperback. The origin of the most successful of these megasellers, Mario Puzo's *The Godfather*, is legendary. As the author later recalled: 'I was 45 years old. I owed $20,000 to relatives, finance companies, banks and assorted bookmakers and loan sharks. It was really time to grow up and sell out.' He sold out into new echelons of bestsellerdom. *The Godfather* did for the Mafia what Arthur Hailey had done for airports, even more profitably. And it did so by never mentioning the mob by name, in either novel or film, so as not to offend law-abiding Italo-Americans.

The Godfather went on to sell an unprecedented ten million copies in the US over the following decade. The same threshold was passed, in the same amazingly short period, by Richard Bach's *Jonathan Livingston Seagull* (1970), Peter Blatty's *The Exorcist* (1971), Peter Benchley's *Jaws* (1974), Erich Segal's *Love Story* (1970), and Erica Jong's *Fear of Flying* (1974 – a feminist *Portnoy's Complaint*). Works such as Harper Lee's *To Kill a Mockingbird* (reprinted 1960), thanks to school sales, prescribed to generations of American schoolchildren as a lesson in good citizenship, had cumulatively cleared almost as many copies, but never so quickly.

Where lots of books are sold, good books thrive. As Reagan (always a friend to bestsellers) liked to say, all the boats go up with the rising water. What literary historians would regard as canonical works profited with the 1970s–80s boom. E. L. Doctorow's artful anti-bicentennial, *Ragtime*, was the #1 seller

9. *To Kill a Mockingbird* (1939), first edition

of 1975–6. It scooped literary prizes, as well as the top slot in the charts. Nobel Prize winner Saul Bellow's *Humboldt's Gift* also figured in that year's top ten, as did Judith Rossner's 'feminism is more complicated than Betty Friedan would have us think' melodrama, *Looking for Mr Goodbar*.

The 'quality superseller' was, in succeeding years, a regular feature of the popular market, with titles such as William Styron's *Sophie's Choice* (#2, 1979), Margaret Atwood's *The Handmaid's Tale* (1986), Tom Wolfe's *The Bonfire of the Vanities* (1987), and Salman Rushdie's *The Satanic Verses* (1989). The American literary sensibility had demonstrably not been prostituted by the expanding popularity of popular fiction, or the bestsellingness of bestsellers. The doomsayers were wrong on that score.

The new seriousness

As the country came to terms with its first ever defeat in war – by 'irregulars' in black pyjamas – America's top novel of 1977 was Leon Uris's *Trinity*. The novel was also a favourite novel of IRA internees at Long Kesh: Bobby Sands, as he starved himself to death in 1981, would read the novel aloud to his fellow internees. It added considerably to their suffering, they later recorded; Jack Higgins's 'Dillon' thrillers were more to their taste. Uris's soggy saga of Irish freedom-fighting sold twice as many as Harold Robbins's *roman-à-clef* about Jacqueline Susann, *Lonely Lady*. 'Serious' was the flavour of the time. John Le Carré's *The Honourable Schoolboy* reached #4 the same year, expressing as it did a growing moral exhaustion with the Cold War.

The late 1970s were good for the imported British product, particularly spy and counterspy thrillers, and 1978 saw another *annus mirabilis*, with Graham Greene's *The Human Factor*, Ken Follett's *The Eye of the Needle*, and several further Le Carré titles. Over this same period, the more robustly optimistic Frederick Forsyth was selling more strongly in the US than his native UK;

this line of gritty spy or special agent thriller was very much a British specialism to American taste. A novel like *Day of the Jackal* 'worked', by virtue of its seeming only too plausible, and was perhaps more appropriately 'faction'. Robert Ludlum's 'paranoid thrillers', with their wild fantasies about underground conspiracy, were, by comparison, over the top.

At the heart of the bestseller machine there had emerged in the late 1970s and 1980s a nucleus of novelists who could, for the first time in American book-trade history, clear a million copies in hardback in a year, at full retail price, and then come back and do it the next year with a new title (while its predecessor went on to sell ten million in paperback). They were headed by Stephen King, who had come on the scene, inauspiciously, with *Carrie* in 1974. He did not stay inauspicious. King's reliably prodigious output over the next quarter of a century would establish him as the 20th-century Edgar Allan Poe, a master of horror, and an unmatched money machine for whichever publisher could outbid the other for his services.

Others in the top division of authors who could sell as many in hardback as bestselling authors of the 1960s in paperback were: James A. Michener (maker of grandiose epics), Jean M. Auel (creator of an unusual string of prehistoric sagas, beginning with *The Clan of the Cave Bear*, #1, 1980), Robert Ludlum (master of the 'paranoid' thriller), and Danielle Steel (writer of women's romance that men read as well).

In 1984, Tom Clancy came to the fore with his Cold War technothriller, *The Hunt for Red October*. This tale of a state-of-the-art Soviet submarine gone rogue and seeking sanctuary in the US was initially published by the Naval Academy Press in Annapolis, so offputtingly technical was it thought to be by commercial houses. However, the public loved it, and – momentously – so did President Reagan. Clancy is plausibly credited with having excited his paramount leader with the '600-warship' doctrine that helped bankrupt the USSR into collapse. Clancy would, thereafter, top the bestseller lists with everything he wrote. With that strange radar which popular novelists sometimes have, he forecast 9/11 in *Executive Orders* (#2, 1996).

What was most noticeable was the 'bankability' of this golden nucleus. In 1987, for example, the first three titles (all selling over a million in $20 hardback) were: King's *The Tommyknockers*, Clancy's *Patriot Games*, and Steel's *Kaleidoscope*. King backed up his top title with *Misery* (#4) and Steel with *Fine Things* (#8). In succeeding years there would be no oddity in finding a couple of Steels, Kings, or Clancys in the same year's lists. Although as big a hitter, title for title, Auel was less prolific.

Tie-ins

With *The Silence of the Lambs* (1988), Thomas Harris laid the way for what would be the most successful thriller-movie tie-in ever. His monstrous master criminal, Dr Hannibal Lecter, became as mythically famous in the popular mind as Dracula, or Frankenstein. By the time of *Hannibal Rising* (conceived simultaneously as film and novel) in 2007, Harris's psychopathic monster (introduced as a marginal presence in *Red Dragon*, 1981), voted by the American Film Institute 'the most memorable villain in film history', was the biggest popular fiction money machine since Sherlock Holmes.

More fluently than Harris – a notoriously costive writer – John Grisham patented with *The Firm* (1991) a conveyor-belt line of legal thrillers which in turn generated an unbroken string of hugely successful, big box-office film adaptations. The undercurrent of liberal idealism in his narratives rendered them attractive to readers who, normally, had little time for courtroom crusaders. President Clinton liked them; Grisham was his Clancy. Clinton also relished, equally tellingly, the Los Angeles-based detective stories of the African American Walter Mosley. Clinton was, Toni Morrison (bestselling author of *Beloved*, 1987) claimed, America's 'first black president', with bedside reading to match.

By the end of the 1990s, Grisham could be banked on to sell two million in hardback, five times as many within a couple of years in paperback, boosted by a movie which would bring in $100m at the box office. In 2005, Grisham's *The Broker* topped both the hardcover and mass-market paperback bestseller lists – a first.

Unlike King – who tried Dickensian serialization (*The Green Mile*), e-fiction (*The Plant*), and, interestingly, ex-generic themes (e.g. spousal battery in *Rose Madder*) – Grisham never deviated far from the Grisham formula, other, that is, than for his bestselling novella, *Skipping Christmas* (2001) – another #1 title, inevitably.

Michael Crichton, as highly trained a scientist as Grisham is a lawyer, pulled off the same trick with his heavily researched hi-tech thrillers – most spectacularly *Jurassic Park* (1990; filmed by Steven Spielberg in 1993), a scientific romance which combined the pulpy thrills of Burroughs's Ape Man with incidental tutorials on Chaos Theory and Stephen Jay Gould's punctuational model of evolution. Crichton's fiction came embellished with learned bibliographies, not so much to instruct as to impress.

Unlike Grisham, Crichton could, occasionally, miss the mark. *Jurassic Park* broke records; *Congo* (a fantasia on much the same Darwinian themes) flopped, and, along with Arthur Herzog's *The Swarm*, inspired what is consistently voted one of the most enjoyable screen turkeys in the history of cinema.

These three chart-topping novelists all multiplied their sales from the synergies of film-and-book, book-and-film reciprocity. So much so that it was suspected that there was what the trade called 'wag the dog' at work – novels, that is, were conceived first as scenarios and screenplays.

One of the threshold moments in the history of American popular fiction in the 20th century was *The Omen* in 1976. David Seltzer did both film screenplay and simultaneously released 'novelization'. The one broke box-office records, the other made #1 on the bestseller list. Seltzer also made the novelization (as practised by such masters of the art as Alan Dean Foster) critically respectable.

New accents, new markets

Feminism made a dent on the tough surface of the crime novel with Sara Paretsky's V. I. Warshawski, introduced with *Indemnity Only* (1982), and Sue Grafton's Kinsey Milhone, introduced in the same year with *A is for Alibi*. Women, like Captain Kirk, had boldly gone where only the male writer had gone before: into Planet Macho ('Kinsey? – isn't that a man's name?').

It was Patricia D. Cornwell, with her Chief Medical Examiner, Kay Scarpetta, introduced with *Post-Mortem* (1990), who would sell most copies and earn the highest advances ever paid a woman novelist in US book-trade annals. Scarpetta, typically, does not investigate crimes, she investigates (in great anatomical detail) the corpse left behind by crime: hers is the romance of the autopsy, formaldehyde fiction. By the turn of the century, Cornwell was topping bestseller lists: a relatively rare achievement for crime fiction. Genre was no longer – or no longer entirely – ghettoized.

New markets emerged, and were exploited, in the late 20th century. Young readers had more disposable income than at any time in American history. V. C. Andrews's strange amalgam of horror and domesticity, which began with *Flowers in the Attic* in 1979, successfully targeted a teen-aged, mainly female, constituency. The novel was a mixture of Anne Frank, de Sade, Louisa May Alcott, and something idiosyncratically nasty. The cocktail was immensely popular. By the late 1990s, Andrews's novels (some of them produced after her death in 1986, but under her franchised brand-name) had sold 100 million copies worldwide.

An even younger readership (or viewership) made William Kotzwinkle's novelization *ET: The Extraterrestrial* the #1 title of 1982 and *The Return of the Jedi Storybook* the #1 title a year later. But, as with genre, the readership was no longer ghettoized: adults read them as they patronized the same McDonald's as their children and scoffed the same Big Macs, fries, and shakes. The pattern would be repeated with Harry Potter, Terry Pratchett, and Philip Pullman. Categories were melting and reforming. A tenth-grader might return from high-school having studied *The Catcher in the Rye*, or *Beloved*, in class and find mom reading *Harry Potter and the Half-Blood Prince*.

Rowling's universal appeal caused some embarrassment. In 2001, the *New York Times*, the most relied-upon list in the US, allegedly created a new category – 'Children's Books' – 'in order to move the Harry Potter books out of the No. 1, 2, and 3 positions on their Fiction chart, where they had remained for over a year'.

New millenarianism

As the new millennium approached, the top of the lists took on a distinctly millenarian flavour. In 1999, the fifth instalment of Jerry Jenkins's and Tim La Haye's twelve-part *Left Behind* fictionalization of the Book of Revelation, *Apollyon: The Destroyer is Unleashed*, came in at #7 on the list, selling something over a million copies. The series had begun with *Left Behind: A Novel of the Earth's Last Days* in 1995, with the pious aim of completing at the crack of doom – the new millennium. The last volume would, as promised by St John, coincide with the Second Coming of Christ (but why not make a few bucks in between?).

The series was hugely boosted by the newly assembled faithful in the 'digital cathedral' and – like *Ben Hur* before it – by mass

purchase and distribution through evangelical organizations
and churches in sympathy with the authors' uncompromising
eschatology. With George W. Bush in the White House, the
religious right now comprised a readership (and a political lobby)
infinitely more sophisticated than the suckers Sinclair Lewis had
satirized in *Elmer Gantry*, or the faithful to whom Udell had
preached.

The Jenkins-La Haye series went from strength to strength,
sales swelling as the end of days approached. In the year 2000,
there were two *Left Behind* titles in the top ten (at #2 and #4)
with combined sales of 4.5 million. And in 2001 (ominous year),
Desecration topped the list, and was the most-read novel in
America. Alas, the Lord was not among those queuing up to read
it. Apocalypse was, apparently, not now. Again.

The *Left Behind* prophetic novels set up a fascinating polarity with
Arthur C. Clarke's techno-utopian (and wholly secular) *2001, A
Space Odyssey*. For Clarke, a cosmic humanist, the 'Apollo mission'
to the planets and beyond, was God. For the theologians La Haye
and Jenkins, Apollyon was Satan.

The religious theme was exploited, with a more perverse spin,
by Dan Brown's *The Da Vinci Code* in 2003, a novel whose plot
is oddly (and certainly accidentally) reminiscent of Guy Thorne's
bestseller *When it was Dark* (discussed in the next chapter). In
Brown's thriller, a Harvard symbologist is charged, against the
massed and unscrupulous power of the Vatican's hit squad Opus
Dei, with decoding the Renaissance painting, buried within whose
iconography is 'proof' that the Gospels are lies. Brown's book went
on to be the biggest bestseller in the century or so since accurate
accountancy was introduced into the retail book trade.

The first decade of the 21st century sees growth on all fronts. More
titles are published, more copies are sold, new genres appear, and
the balance of power between the genres constantly fluctuates.

Science fiction is somewhat in retreat and fantasy ascendant. The western, despite a 'new western' blip in the 1970s, is no longer tall in the saddle. Crime fiction burgeons, as, alas, does crime; both have diversified.

Alongside the 'bankable' quartet (Grisham, King, Steel, Clancy) are James Patterson and J. K. Rowling. The former turns out a novel a year, often with an (unmemorable) collaborator, and had no fewer than five titles in the 2005 list. He does not write novels, he has explained, he 'sheds' them. J. K. Rowling, the other pre-potent regular producer, brings out an inevitably record-breaking instalment of the Potter saga every few years. The Hannibal Lecter franchise thrives. And, from time to time, very good books (as the critics would think) make the lists, if only to confound cultural pessimists.

Over the long term, all that can be said with certainty is (1) there will be more bestsellers; (2) they will sell ever better; (3) they will defy prediction.

Chapter 5
The British bestseller

Prehistory

British bestsellerism is rooted in different cultural and commercial subsoil from America's. Britain has always preserved a higher retail cost for new books: protected formally, for a hundred years after the 1890s, by the NBA. Educational and class systems have been other differentiating factors.

None the less, one perceives the same large shapes. One-off bestsellers, those that sell fastest, tend to be short-lived. And there is a polarity between these solo, short-life blockbusters and bestselling lines of fiction to which habituated readers are 'genre-loyal', often over many years.

There were bestsellers before bestseller lists, just as there were 'novels' before that term came into use. Samuel Richardson's enthusiastic admirers ('Pamela-ites') prefigure innumerable subsequent enthusiasms. From the first, one sees cult practices clustered around wildly popular works of fiction, such as Goethe's *The Sorrows of Young Werther* (1742; canary-yellow trousers and an epidemic of adolescent suicide), Bulwer's *Pelham* (1828; dark suits and Byronic scowls for men), or du Maurier's *Trilby* (1894; the ever popular felt hat).

The formative move towards the modern system, the bestseller 'machine', arrived with Walter Scott. Allied with the genius of the Scottish publisher Archibald Constable, every new *Waverley* novel constituted, as Sydney Smith jested, a 'holiday for the nation'.

Constable promoted Scott's fiction with a brilliant sales 'stunt'. For a decade, as they came out, sometimes as many as three a year, the *Waverley* novels were issued as from the pen of the 'Great Unknown'. Who was the mysterious author? *Aut Walter Scott aut Diaboli*, said Maria Edgeworth. But who could be sure? Curiosity, whatever it may do for cats, sells novels.

The science of 'puffing' ('log-rolling', 'hype') was patented in the 1820s by Henry Colburn – the 'Prince of Puffers'. He would, for example, hint that such-and-such a novel issued from an 'eminent hand' whose owner, for obvious reasons, could not be named. Or, in one notorious case, that the novel had been found on a bloodstained pillow.

Colburn 'made' Disraeli (*Vivien Gray*, 1827), Lady Morgan (*The Wild Irish Girl*, 1806), and Bulwer Lytton (lordly master of all genres). The last of these bestselling authors (all of whom despised Colburn for the hucksterism that made them bestsellers) fantasized how the Prince of Puffers would have dealt with the apostles, had they brought their gospel manuscripts to his Conduit Street establishment.

Outside Mayfair, the reading public of the slums was catered to by 'penny dreadfuls'. Printed on pulp, with crude woodcut illustrations, and not too many long words, publishers such as Edward Lloyd ran off serials by the million. 'Classics' (loosely used) of the penny dreadful genre are J. M. Rymer's captivity narrative, *Ada the Betrayed* (1845) and Thomas Prest's *A String of Pearls* (1846), better known by its theatrical title, *Sweeney Todd: The Demon Barber of Fleet Street* (don't eat that meat pie).

In the mid-century, with growth in national literacy, George Routledge's 'railway fiction' diffused popular fiction across the country's transport network. None the less, the middle-class, educated elite remained a fairly small readership. Dickens, the 'great inimitable', averaged about 50,000 for monthly sales of his serialized novels.

Britain did not merely have a smaller population and landmass than America, it had a less literate general reading public and a more powerful elite within that public. Throughout most of the century, one perceives a deep cultural fissure in popular reading. The middle and upper classes borrowed their fiction, respectably bound, from Mr Mudie or Mr Smith, or their local circulating library. The 'people' devoured their slum literature for half-pence, and then hung it in the privy.

The market for fiction received a huge boost, and some pressure towards homogenization, from the 1870 Universal Education Act. But the stratification persisted. In the 1890s, high-brows and middle-brows, for example, had Sherlock Holmes, popularized in Newnes's *Strand Magazine* (a slick, sixpenny production, to which Queen Victoria herself contributed). A 'new Holmes' could drive circulation up to half a million.

Low-brows had Sexton Blake, 'the office boys' Sherlock Holmes', as Dorothy L. Sayers (creator of Lord Peter Wimsey – 'the toffs' Holmes') called him. Blake began crime-busting in 1893, in the *Halfpenny Marvel*. Unattached like Holmes to any one author's life span, he was still busting away in the 1970s, supported by his 'Watson' Tinker, and his bloodhound Pedro. 'Blakes' were written by as many as 125 pseudonymous and anonymous authors over the years, the young John Creasey being among the more famous.

The Sexton Blake factory (eventually owned by Northcliffe's Amalgamated Press) was merely doing what Edward Lloyd's 'Salisbury Square' hacks had done with their plagiarisms of

Dickens (e.g. 'The Nickwick Papers') in the 1840s. But, as the century drew to its close, the hacks were doing their hackwork more efficiently, as what Wilkie Collins had called the 'unknown public' ('a public to be counted by the millions') drifted upwards into more literate, less heavily populated middle-brow territory.

As the popular fiction industry sales increased, so did leading authors' payments. By the end of the century, Marie Corelli, Mrs Humphry Ward, George du Maurier, and Hall Caine were earning up to £10,000 for superselling works such as *Trilby*, *Eleanor*, *The Sorrows of Satan*, and *The Manxman*. These five-figure sums equate into the seven figures Jeffrey Archer can nowadays expect; it was big business.

With the collapse of the three-volume, or 'library edition', novel in the early 1890s, there was a palpable shift in fiction-reading Britain from a borrowing to a buying culture. The new one-volume novel, at 6s – with cheaper reprints in hot pursuit – was aggressively marketed by 'new' publishers such as Chatto & Windus and Methuen. The 'single-decker' was retailed both to purchasers and to opportunistic corner shop 'tupenny' lending libraries.

Corelli was the most flamboyant of the 1890s top-sellers. She was also the most aggressive in tangling with fellow authors, whom she (correctly) suspected despised her. *Barabbas* (1893), with its preposterous 'Judith Iscariot', was a hit against Mrs Humphry Ward's *Robert Elsmere*, and, in the market place, it was an even greater hit than Ward's high-toned piety. In *The Sorrows of Satan* (1895), Corelli invents a novelist-hero who makes a Faustian pact with the devil, who can have his soul in return for a bestseller or two. So much for George Gissing's mournful plaint about the woes of authorship in *New Grub Street* (1891).

The more 'realistic' Hall Caine drew his inspiration from Victor Hugo, rather than Corelli's mentor, Bulwer Lytton. Caine's tribute to his birthplace, *The Manxman* (1894), sold a reputed half million by 1900. In 1901, riding the millenarian wave, Caine brought out his great work, *The Eternal City*. It foresees a republic, in 1950, whose charter is the Lord's Prayer. As one reviewer put it: 'to enter Mr Caine's city is rather like plunging into a vast cauldron of primitive hotchpotch'. Hotchpotch sold like hot cakes. *The Eternal City* is reputedly the first 'fast-seller' in British popular fiction to clear a million copies in a couple of years. On his munificent royalties, Caine became a royal figure on his island, emerging from his castle to dazzle the Manx natives in his chauffeur-driven Rolls Royce. He left a quarter of a million pounds on his death in 1931.

Hall Caine and Corelli sold massively in America; as did du Maurier with *Trilby*, his prudently Anglicized *vie bohème*. 'Kailyard' (i.e. cabbage patch) also exported well to America. The leader in the genre was Ian Maclaren, with his *Beside the Bonnie Brier Bush* (1894), which was a top title in Peck's 'first ever' American bestseller list in 1895. Alternately cloyingly sentimental and pawkily comic, Maclaren's novel is a bundle of sketches of life in 'Drumtochty', Perthshire. Maclaren had another Kailyard novel in the same 1895 list, *Days of Auld Lang Syne* (# 6). When not writing fiction, Maclaren was the Revd. John Watson, a douce minister.

America was Scottish-mad; English, slightly less so. London, however, preferred the less pietistic master of Kailyard, J. M. Barrie, whose 'Thrums' stories launched his career in fiction and lent themselves to adaptation on the West End stage (and, later, Hollywood).

Edwardian favourites

Britain – while greedily devouring American bestsellers – had its local favourites, less admired in the US market. H. G. Wells was never taken up massively in the US. Nor, in his early (and best) popular fiction, was Somerset Maugham, whose semi-autobiographical *Of Human Bondage* (1915) sold powerfully in the UK but made little dent on the bestseller list in America until the 1934 film (which, coincidentally, launched the career of Bette Davis).

Conan Doyle certainly appealed to the American mass market: with series heroes such as Sherlock Holmes, Brigadier Gerard, and Professor Challenger (e.g. *The Lost World*, 1912) titles. But folkloric as his heroes became, Doyle never enjoyed the pre-1914 success in the US of Jeffery Farnol, W. J. Locke, or Mrs Humphry Ward.

Guy Thorne's *When it was Dark* was the runaway hit of 1903 in Britain. A professor, expert in biblical archaeology, is dispatched to the Holy Land to decipher a document 'proving' that the resurrection never happened. Society, as the Edwardians knew it, falls apart (contemporary readers may observe similarities with a bestseller of exactly 100 years on, Dan Brown's *The Da Vinci Code* (2003) – something very strange happens to reading publics as the millennium turns).

The Bishop of London pontificated solemnly about Thorne's novel in Westminster Abbey. Decades later, General Montgomery of Alamein cited it as the novel that had changed his life. (A similar claim was made by Graham Greene about Marjorie Bowen's 1908 romance, *The Viper of Milan*. As with Monty, the novel had a strong, if indirect, effect on his adult religious convictions.)

Equally dotty was M. P. Shiel's bestseller, *The Lord of the Sea* (1901), written in a frenzy of xenophobic alarm at Jewish refugees 'swamping' into England and taking the country over. The narrative ends with the hero setting up a fleet of huge 'sea fortresses' to protect his green and pleasant land, having appointed himself 'King Richard of Seas'. Like his lion-hearted namesake, he issues anti-Jewish decrees from his flag-fort Boodah; England may sleep safely.

Prejudice sold novels – by the ton. So did romance and exotic settings. The biggest by far Edwardian 'bigseller' (as they were then called) was *The Blue Lagoon* (1908), by an author with the Wodehousian name H. De Vere Stacpoole. In Stacpoole's Robinsoniad two eight-year-olds, Dickie and Emmeline, are shipwrecked on a desert island. Over the (blissful) years, they discover the arts of survival and the delights – somewhat below the age of consent – of 'the endless kiss'. And, for reasons they can never quite fathom, parenthood.

Stacpoole's South Seas idyll is a *ne plus ultra* of Edwardian escapism. It is also an exemplary case of how popular novels take in each other's washing. The basic premise goes back via Ballantyne's *The Coral Island* to Crusoe's primal marooning. More recently, it draws on E. Nesbit's *The Railway Children* (1906), and its three children who are abandoned, adultless, at Three Chimneys Cottage. James Hilton's Shangri La, in *Lost Horizon*, is a Blue Lagoon in the Himalayas. Elements of 'Blue Lagoonism' resurface, in reversed form, in *Lord of the Flies* and can even be detected in the 2004 television series *Lost*.

In Robert Hichens's *Garden of Allah* (1905), the reader might, for a mere six-bob, escape to the burning sands of the East. Hichens's Saharan romance is permeated with the religious flavour found in many Edwardian bestsellers (the title alludes to the Arabian proverb – which may well be as Arabian as bangers and mash – that 'the desert is the Garden of Allah').

The 'tramp novel' offered less far-flung escapism; gentlemen of the road could be seen from the front window of every terrace house. The 'happy tramp' formula was patented by W. J. Locke in *The Beloved Vagabond* (1906). The 'vagabond' (so much nicer a word than 'vagrant') of Locke's title is a 'wandering philosopher', Berzelius Nibbibard Paragot, a wine-loving Gascon who philosophizes (interminably) about life, and the glorious freedom of tramping. (The novel is satirized by E. M. Forster in Leonard Bast's moonlight walk in *Howards End*, 1910.)

Locke was as popular in the US as in the UK, regularly topping pre-war lists, and this popularity accounted for his princely income, reckoned at £15,000 per year. This, during the period when Lloyd George introduced the first old age pension: 5s a week for over-70s. The 'jolly tramp' theme was later exploited by Wells in works such as *The History of Mr Polly* (1910) and, more remuneratively, by Jeffery Farnol in *The Broad Highway* (also 1910). The early 19th-century setting of Farnol's novel also popularized what would later be known as 'Regency romance' – a genre subsequently distinguished by Georgette Heyer, crudified by Barbara Cartland, and mass marketed to this day by Mills & Boon.

Like Locke, Farnol was phenomenally popular in the US, where *The Broad Highway* was the bestselling American novel of 1911. But the biggest seller of the decade, on both sides of the Atlantic, was Florence Barclay's *The Rosary* (1909). The wife of a clergyman, dedicated to good works in London's East End, Barclay suffered a health crisis in the 1890s and took to writing fiction. *The Rosary* was inspired by a popular song. Does Gareth *really* love her, wonders the Hon. Jane Champion? She discovers the truth when he is blinded, and she nurses him, *incognita*. *The Rosary* sold 150,000 copies in its first year in the UK and topped the American bestseller list in 1910. So remunerative was it in America that the publisher, Putnam, renamed their building 'The Rosary'. On her part, the pious Barclay donated her huge earnings to charity.

World War I and popular fiction

Notably less to American taste than Barclay (until Hollywood took him up) was A. E. W. Mason, whose *The Four Feathers* (1902) chronicles the abject cowardice and redeeming bravery of Harry Feversham in the Sudan. The death-or-glory militarism glamorized by Mason came under strain the following decade, in World War I – even if the white feather his novel had made iconic figured prominently on the home front. Fevershams died by the million, for what?

Theirs not to question why. During the war, spirits were kept up by works such as Ian Hay's docufictional *The First Hundred Thousand* (if only casualties had stuck at that 1914 level). So successful in the US was Hay's account of Albion's girding itself for war that the War Department dispatched the author there, to propagandize for his country alongside Hall Caine (whose efforts, he unpatriotically complained, cost him $150,000 in lost earnings).

Anti-war sentiment combined with postwar disillusionment in A. S. M. Hutchinson's phenomenally successful *If Winter Comes* (1921) – a prime example of what the Germans called *Heimatkehrliteratur* (returned-home novels). Hutchinson's book, which sold 100,000 copies in its first year in Britain, was the #1 title of 1922 in America. Clergymen gave sermons on ex-officer Mark Sabre's plight in a postwar world of cads, lounge-lizards, soft-faced profiteers, scrimshankers, and shrewish, less than faithful wives.

The genre would reach even higher levels of bestsellerdom with Warwick Deeping's *Sorrell and Son* (1925), in which an ex-officer, to give his son a gent's education, takes up work as a hotel porter. No medals for that kind of gallantry.

The soldier's tale still retained its glamour, so long as it was far away from the trenches. P. C. Wren's *Beau Geste* (1924) had gone through 51 English editions by 1960. The most enduringly popular, and much-filmed, of the 'Foreign Legion' novels, it recycled Ouida's 1867 bestseller *Under Two Flags* and drew on Hichens's 'burning sands' mystique for readers who would, in their actual lives, get no closer to the Sahara than Margate beach.

Those Saharan sands burned even more erotically in Edith M. Hull's phenomenally successful *The Sheik* (1921), whose romance Wren set out to correct with some masculine factuality.

Wren incarnates the wilfully philistine tinge of many interwar British bestsellers. As he complacently observed: 'The bulk of my readers are cleanly-minded virile outdoor sort of people, of both sexes ... I am not a "professional novelist", nor, a long-haired literary cove.' The shock waves from the Oscar Wilde trials in the 1890s can still be felt in such protestations of 'normality'.

Cosmopolitan sophistication of a kind was offered by Michael Arlen (Dikran Kouyoumdjian) in *The Green Hat* (1925), whose daring 'syphilis in high places' theme reputedly earned him half a million pounds. On the strength of the novel's success, Arlen moved to Hollywood in the mid-1920s. He is remembered, if at all, as 'Michaelis' in *Lady Chatterley's Lover*.

British genre

In the early 20th century, Britain could claim world leadership in a number of fictional genres. They included, to list summarily, seven:

(1) the governess novel, whose greatest post-Brontean exponent would be Victoria Holt/Jean Plaidy;

(2) the Saharan romance, as exemplified by Robert Hichens and Edith M. Hull;

(3) the Ruritanian romance, invented by Anthony Hope, with *The Prisoner of Zenda* (1894), and brought to its highest pitch in Eric Ambler's *The Mask of Dimitrios* (1939);

(4) the powder and wig romance, a kind of male Regency fiction, first popularized by Stanley Weyman, and exploited most successfully by Hugh Walpole, in his *Rogue Herries* series;

(5) the soil and gloom romance, pioneered by Mary Webb (*Gone to Earth*, 1917; *Precious Bane*, 1924) and affectionately burlesqued by Stella Gibbons in *Cold Comfort Farm* (1933);

(6) the buccaneering romance: the master of this genre was Rafael Sabatini with works such as *The Sea Hawk* (1915) and, pre-eminently, *Captain Blood: His Odyssey* (1922), nominated by George Macdonald Fraser as 'one of the great unrecognized novels of the twentieth century', although the Errol Flynn-starring film of 1935 may not have helped it be recognized as such;

(7) the Mills & Boon romance: the publisher launched their line of books for women in the 1920s, every volume centring around the inexhaustibly fascinating 'great husband hunt'. Among the many writers for the imprint, the name of Ruby M. Ayres stands out; writing four a novels a year, and a lifetime total of 150 titles (beginning with *Castles in Spain*, in 1912), Ayres is reckoned to have sold some ten million copies.

All these genres, and others, thrived, and recruited millions of readers. But the most critically respected interwar genre in Britain was the 'golden-age' detective novel, dominated by country houses, whimsical sleuthing lords, Holmesian amateurs, and cyanide in the tea-leaves. The 'Queen' of the genre was Agatha Christie. Her first, precociously accomplished novel, *The Mysterious Affair at Styles*, was written in 1916, on leave from war-time nursing. It introduced a refugee detective from plucky little Belgium, Hercule Poirot. He would remain, clearing things up in country houses, long after his own country was liberated.

'Cosies', as they were called (after the woollen warmers put on teapots), would become ever more ingenious, with the authors' 'Detective Club' devising rules and setting standards of writerly and readerly skill. Cosiness is likewise the climate of Dornford Yates's *Berry and Co.* (1920). The ensuing 'Berry Books' take the form of an extended string of stories about a 'happy family', the Pleydells, in their country house 'White Ladies', Hants. Loosely structured and ironic in tone, the Berry saga, whose span extends from 1907 to 1950, celebrates the indestructability of British gentry and their capacity to survive the Kaiser, world slump, and Hitler. But a Labour government? Some things defeat even the Berry family.

Thrillerdom

Yates also pioneered the 'clubland thriller' genre with his series hero, William Chandos. The series began with *Blind Corner* (1927). Cheek by jowl with Sapper's upper-class thug, 'Bulldog' Drummond, Chandos represents a distinctively British line of 'snobbery with violence'. As Yates's series opens, Chandos has recently been sent down from Oxford for beating up some communists. Bulldog's violence is directed, typically, against cosmopolitan Jews. As with their lineal descendant, James Bond, saving England from the un-English is the great project.

John Creasey – the most prolific of the clubland hero practitioners, with some 600 titles to his credit – introduced the 'Toff' in 1938. A more likeable chap than the above shiny brutes, the Hon. Richard Rollison is to all appearances a wealthy playboy. But behind that disguise, he is less world-saver than a modern Robin Hood. More in the Baroness Orczy's Scarlet Pimpernel line of 'gentleman avengers' was Leslie Charteris's *The Saint* (alias Simon Templar), introduced in 1928 and still going strong half a century later, boosted by radio, television, and film adaptation.

With *Ashenden*, in 1928, Somerset Maugham created the prototypical spy fiction thriller. The stories were based on the author's own experiences with the newly formed MI6 agency during World War I. Maugham had been, as he drily noted, dispatched single-handed to Russia 'to prevent the Bolshevik Revolution'. 007 might just have pulled it off.

Maugham did not take his highly original ('secret agent') conception forward. The most enduringly successful exponent of the espionage thriller in its early form was the Scot John Buchan. Buchan interspersed a high-flying career in law and government with writing 'shockers', as he called them. *The Thirty-Nine Steps* (1915) launched him into bestselling fame. Four other 'shockers' followed, based on the daring exploits of Richard Hannay, South African mining engineer and ever-ready secret agent. While few remember Buchan as Governor General of Canada, the highpoint of his public service career, his 'Hannay' novels are still in print, and *The Thirty-Nine Steps* is regularly adapted on screen.

The 'thriller' was very much a British specialty between the wars. Outside the clubland ethos were writers with larger constituencies. The largest such (by some reckonings a quarter of the adult population) belonged to Edgar Wallace – a writer whom supporters (many fewer of them nowadays) claim to have invented the thriller genre with *The Four Just Men* (1904). The Four Just Men are a quartet of extraordinarily high-minded, international crusader criminals prepared to stop at nothing (even assassination) to save civilization. The legendarily prolific Wallace also created 'Sanders of the River', a District Commissioner who brings civilization to the heart of darkness with the Gatling Gun. Wallace died in 1932, devising the great ape, King Kong, for Hollywood, with some 175 novels and 160 film adaptations to his credit.

If Wallace was the King, Dennis Wheatley, who arrived on the scene in the 1930s, was the 'Prince of Thrillers'. He too had his four just men, under the leadership of the Duc de Richleau. The quartet, more rabidly anti-Bolshevik than Wallace's, did battle, indefatigably, against the Reds and Nazis in 18 novels. In the 1960s, Wheatley enjoyed a second bestselling career writing satanic thrillers, of which the most famous (thanks largely to the Hammer films) is *The Devil Rides Out*. As a web page devoted to Wheatley ruefully records: 'thirty years after his death [1977], his books have all but disappeared from bookshops. Where, at one time, W. H. Smith displayed shelves of his titles, now there are none.'

Graham Greene (whose books are still very much to be found on the shelves of Waterstone's, if not always Smith's) saw the potential of the thriller market and exploited it with his 1932 'entertainment' *Stamboul Train*. Throughout his career, like Eric Ambler, Greene would cultivate a distinguished line of thriller for more sophisticated readers.

Sump thrillers

There were also plenty of the less distinguished, but even better-selling, kind. Britain had its own version of the 'hard-boiled' crime novel – a field led by Peter Cheyney. East End London to the core (his father ran a fish stall), Cheyney's best-known series hero was the 'G-man' (Yank) hero Lemmy Caution ('Let me caution you'), introduced in *This Man is Dangerous* (1936). At his heyday, in the 1940s, Cheyney was selling over a million copies a year. Although despised by the literary classes in his home country and unknown in America, Cheyney attracted a cultish following among French intellectuals. Jean-Luc Godard's 'New Wave' film, *Alphaville*, for example, features Lemmy Caution as its hero.

The French intelligentsia, for their own inscrutable reasons, also had more time than did George Orwell for James Hadley Chase, whose *No Orchids for Miss Blandish* (1939) – with its American gangster pornography – inspired the famous essay 'Raffles and Miss Blandish'. For Orwell, Chase's bestseller was 'pure Fascism': as dangerous as Hitler, and harder to stop.

Even tackier in the pseudo-American, hard-boiled, poor man's Spillane vein, was Hank Jansen (a pseudonym for many anonymous hands), who came on the scene with *When Dames*

Get Tough (1947). Respectable bookshops would not handle such wares, and they were prosecuted by local magistrates from time to time, but 'Jansens' sold by the hundred thousand through other channels.

Slump fiction

The 1929 crash and subsequent economic slump reverberated through bestselling fiction, as through all areas of British life. It can be felt not merely in works such as Walter Greenwood's *Love on the Dole* (1933), but as a sombre thread in the fabric of (normally cheerful) J. B. Priestley's bestselling serio-comedy of office life in the City of London, *Angel Pavement* (1931). It is a feature of periods of economic slump that popular fiction does well: novels being one of the cheapest luxuries available to a hard-up population with time on its hands. *Angel Pavement*, glum as it might be, did very well for Priestley: 'My golden gusher', he called it. There were few such gushers in England in the 1930s.

Angrier in tone, and broader in social sweep, was the 'British *Grapes of Wrath*', *How Green was my Valley* (1939). Richard Llewellyn's angry saga of coal-miners' hardship in Wales was reprinted 20 times in its first year, echoing as it did the Prince of Wales's despairing: 'something must be done'.

One name dominated as the king of the (British) bestsellers on the eve of war: A. J. Cronin. *The Citadel* (1937), marketed cannily by the publisher Victor Gollancz, went through 14 editions in its first six months. British sales of 304,000 were recorded by 1942. *The Citadel* takes the form of a *Bildungsroman* ('portrait novel'), recounting the career of a Scottish doctor, Andrew Manson, who almost loses his soul to a 'devouring desire for material success'. Will Andy sell his soul to Harley Street and the fashionable doctor's Rolls? Finally (after many travails), the answer is 'no'. With its heroic, embattled young doctor hero, *The Citadel* popularized 'hospital melodrama' in Britain. Echoes can be found in innumerable Mills & Boon romances, television soaps, and even – by a circuitous route – in Richard Gordon's postwar *Doctor in the House* comedies. Cronin's novel, along with his 'Dr Finlay's Casebook' stories, introduced a couple of years earlier, plausibly laid some of the ground for the National Health Service.

The 1940s

Wartime Britain carried on reading pretty much what it had read during the pre-war period and would continue to read for a few years afterwards. There was little choice but mark time, given paper rationing and ministry controls, and the bestseller sector of the book trade stagnated for the duration of the war. The 'fizz' which effervesces the bestseller was necessarily in short supply. 'Blockbuster' brought to mind bombs dropped from Lancaster bombers (or Heinkels, if you were unlucky) rather than novels by Margaret Mitchell. The climate of cultural austerity is caught in the opening chapters of Graham Greene's *End of the Affair* (1951) and, even more vividly, those of Orwell's *Nineteen Eighty-Four* (1949 – the novel is patently about 1948). There are no bestsellers in Winston Smith's Victory Mansions, any more than there is malt whisky in Maurice Bendrix's Windmill pub, at the beginning of Greene's novel.

Paperbacks – notably Penguin and Mills & Boon – thrived during the war. Allen Lane's firm produced a distinguished line of fiction reprints within the restrictive production confines of 'wartime regulations'. In the absence of a large section of the male population, women's romance expanded to fill the vacancy. Georgette Heyer and Barbara Cartland would, during the 1940s, establish themselves as Queens of Regency reigning over two territories: one highland, one lowland.

In the hardback sector, long-established names dominated the 1940s. Cronin, Hilton, du Maurier, Wheatley, H. E. Bates, and Christie are found, year in, year out, in the lists compiled in

W. H. Smith's and the trade papers as 'the books most in demand' in the nation's high street bookshops.

One significant difference (attributable to wartime alliances) was the presence of a more 'literary' vein of American literature. Steinbeck's *The Grapes of Wrath* was among Britain's most bought new novels in 1940. The same author's tale of Scandinavian resistance to Nazi occupation, *The Moon is Down* (1943), also found favour. Ernest Hemingway was, for the first time in Britain, selling more than Dennis Wheatley (for example) with *For Whom the Bell Tolls* (chronicling another war) from 1940 to 1942. The runaway hit in America in the years 1943–5, Lloyd C. Douglas's elaboration of the Gospels, *The Robe*, was a bestseller in the UK, as was Kathleen Winsor's saucy (and comically inaccurate) tale of Restoration romps, *Forever Amber* (1946).

As in America, it was a year or two after hostilities before popular fiction came properly to terms with the war. The home-grown bestseller to do so first was Nevil Shute's POW chronicle, *A Town Like Alice* (1949). According to *Smith's News*, it 'was easily the most successful novel of the year', perhaps because the British population also felt cooped up, if less brutally than by the forces of Nippon.

Whereas American bestselling war fiction concentrated on the experience of infantrymen (*vide* Norman Mailer, James Jones, Irwin Shaw), in Britain it was the Royal Navy, with works such as Nicholas Monsarrat's *The Cruel Sea* (1951) and Alastair MacLean's *HMS Ulysses* (1955). The stress was unrelentingly on the unglamorousness of the conflict at sea. C. S. Forester offered a less recent, but as patriotic, view of nautical life in his 'Hornblower' series, set in the Napoleonic Wars. A 'middie' in 1937, Horatio had made it to Lieutenant by the end of the 1940s, and in time he would rise to the rank of Admiral Hornblower, bringing millions of readers with him.

The 1950s: fiction on the rates

James Bond, introduced to the British reader in 1953 with *Casino Royale*, was also, before joining HM's Secret Service, a Senior Service man. As preparation for his 007 thrillers, Ian Fleming set himself to study such masters as Sapper, Buchan, Cheyney, and Edgar Wallace. Fragments from them all are found floating on the surface of his narratives. The opening line of *Casino Royale* is, however, less clubland than pure snobland: 'The scent and smoke and sweat of a casino are nauseating at three o'clock in a morning.' At this time, BBC-TV (the only choice) signed off at 10 p.m., with the Queen and the Horlicks. To remember what life was like at three o'clock in the morning, most citizens would have had to cast their minds back to wartime and blackout. Bond would save them from that happening again.

Famously, the Bond series got a huge boost when President Kennedy (possibly wishing to distinguish himself from his predecessor, Eisenhower, who favoured Zane Grey) cited Fleming as favourite reading. The first Bond film, in 1962, set a ball rolling which looks as if it will roll forever, even in a Britain that now has its own malodorous supercasinos doing business at 3 a.m.

December 1954 was a prophetic moment in the evolution of British bestsellerism. Orwell's dystopia, *Nineteen Eighty-Four* had been published in 1949, to moderate success. A BBC-TV adaptation, by Nigel Kneale, five years later, made a sensational impact. The 'horror play' was reported to have led to the death by narrative shock of some susceptible viewers witnessing the rodent nightmare that lay behind the door of Room 101. The furore (including questions in Parliament) made Orwell's novel the book of the day. Eventually, 'horrors' notwithstanding, the book would be studied in schools, for the good lessons it offered on citizenship. Over the decades it would sell even more than Bond.

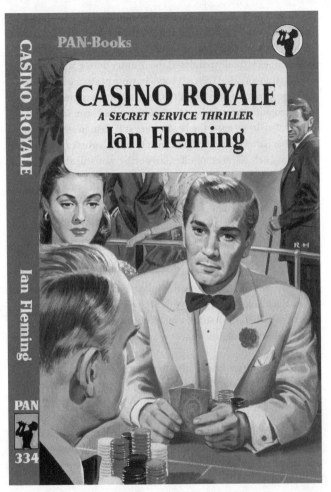

PAN-Books

CASINO ROYALE
A SECRET SERVICE THRILLER
Ian Fleming

CASINO ROYALE

Ian Fleming

PAN
334

10. *Casino Royale*, a mass-market paperback edition from the 1960s

The buried bestseller, exhumed and reanimated by television treatment, was even more graphically demonstrated by John Galsworthy's 1920s *Forsyte Saga*. Serialized in 1967, the programmes virtually paralysed the country during their Sunday evening transmission (church services were postponed to allow congregations to watch). By 1970, over a million copies of the reprinted, nine-strong 'Forsyte Chronicles' had been sold (happily for the novelist's estate, the books were still, just, in copyright). The same pattern was repeated with Robert Graves's *I, Claudius* and its sequels (Graves, unlike Galsworthy, was still alive to profit).

Britain's postwar welfare state had extended its benign tentacles into the provision of entertaining fiction for the population. Public libraries were, during the 1940s and 1950s, a primary source of supply for new hardback novels. 'Fiction on the Rates', it was called. This state of affairs was cemented further by the 1959 Roberts Act, which guaranteed a 'full and efficient' library service across the whole country. As with Mudie's Circulating Library, a century earlier, the market was tilted away from buying to borrowing its popular fiction.

The public library ethos, while offering a generous selection of reading matter (a standard six books every fortnight), encouraged sedateness of choice. Readers, with the privilege of acquiring new novels by the armful, became brand loyal. They would 'take out' or 'reserve' the latest Christie, Forester, Mazo de la Roche, Alastair MacLean, or Hammond Innes for no other reason than that they had so liked the previous ones. Authors reciprocated by bringing out a new title, not too different from the last title, every year or so. There was little pressure from P2P (producer to purchaser) advertising, as it is now called. This was a significant difference between the British and American systems. Whereas a bulk of advertising in America was directed towards the book-buying consumer, in Britain it tended to be localized in trade journals, in which the publisher would attempt to persuade the retailer what to stock, or the librarian what to acquire for their shelves.

Cosiness even infected that most insubordinate of genres, science fiction. John Wyndham had notable success with his 'cosy catastrophes' (as fellow science fiction writer Brian Aldiss wittily labelled them). *The Day of the Triffids* (1951) opens with a mass blinding of the British population by mysterious glinting satellites – probably Russian, perhaps American. The country is then terrorized by giant, genetically modified mangelwurzels: a peculiarly British disaster.

In Wyndham's *The Kraken Wakes* (1953), Stacpoole's giant octopus from *The Blue Lagoon*, magnified a thousandfold, emerges from the deep to finish the job Hitler started. Typically, Wyndham's scenarios end with the surviving happy family stronger and happier than ever. His science fiction did for the genre what Bradbury was doing in the United States: he took it out of the genre ghetto. Fans rather despised Wyndham for the reason that non-fans liked him. J. G. Ballard's extremely un-cosy catastrophe fantasies, such as *The Drowned World* (1962), which current geo-climatic events have, alas, proved more prophetic than Wyndham's, were less to the public taste, although connoisseurs of the genre rated them as among the best examples of science fiction.

Angry Young Men

The cosy cultural climate, and the social conformity that underlay it (a hangover from wartime collectivism), was challenged with the irruption of the 'Angry Young Men' in the early and mid-1950s. Whether satirical like Kingsley Amis's pioneering campus novel *Lucky Jim* (1954), or furiously resentful like John Braine's *Room at the Top* (1957; selling an amazing 5,000 copies in its first week), the movement was defiantly 'bolshy' – without, however, formulating any clear political position. The inflamed mood of the 'angries' was summed up by Alan Sillitoe's working-class hero, Arthur Seaton, in *Saturday Night and Sunday Morning* (1958): 'and trouble for me it'll be, fighting every day until I die'.

The Angry Young Men movement paralleled that of the Beatniks in the US, with the difference that the American 'angries', as witnessed in Jack Kerouac's *On the Road* (1957), were more prone to drop out than rebel. There is a telling moment at the end of Keith Waterhouse's *Billy Liar* (1959; boosted by the 1963 film and the 1970s television series) in which the hero almost plucks up courage to leave his provincial northern town and go down to the 'Smoke', but loses his nerve at the last minute. It is a symptomatic loss of nerve which Sal Paradise would never have succumbed to. Arthur Seaton finally settles down and marries; Joe Lampton sells his soul for membership of the Conservative Club and a Jaguar. Anger was, ultimately, a spasm not the prelude to any kind of effective rebellion or mould-breaking. But anger sold books, and recruited young readers.

The special relationship

A number of factors tended, over the next few decades, to draw Britain and America closer together in their popular reading preferences. An infrastructural factor was the erosion, and eventual abolition, of the 'Traditional Market Agreement' which had divided the globe up into zones of international copyright monopoly. Effectively, the TMA had given the British publishing industry preferential rights in large, Anglophone territories. With the TMA's disappearance, American books became a larger presence worldwide, and in the UK, to which they were now aggressively exported.

A second factor was the 'paperback revolution' of the 1960s (following the 'Lady Chatterley' breakthrough) which brought with it a mass of imported titles from America.

A third factor was the 'agglomeration' of the British and American publishing industries into ever larger, and eventually multinational, combines. It resulted in a series of yokings emblematized in the currently largest British (so to call it) imprint, HarperCollins: in geographical terms, as schizoid a term as 'LondonNewYork'.

A fourth, and clinching, factor was the installation of bestseller lists at the centre of the British retail trade, after decades of resistance, in the mid-1970s. Together with the increasing cosmopolitanism of the population – free to travel, at last, without 'currency controls' – and the saturation of British culture by American television and film imports, a hybridized, and mid-Atlanticized, picture emerges in the consumption of popular fiction in the two principal English-speaking markets.

But, increasingly, as in most relationships, one party came to dominate. The first American lists in the 1890s had been dominated by British imports. By 2000, it was common to see not a single British title in the American weekly bestseller lists – despite the huge popularity of novelists such as Rowling or J. R. R. Tolkien (whose posthumous career as a bestseller had begun in the US, in the hippy 1960s). Meanwhile, American novels would be conspicuous in the British lists.

The drift, continued over decades, was towards pan-Americanization. By the turn of the century, bestselling novelists such as Stephen King would schedule authors' tours to Britain as routinely as to California. The UK, however, retained bestselling strong points. The spy, or counter-spy, novel – laced with male action – was one. John Le Carré's anti-Bond, *The Spy Who Came in from the Cold* (1963), set the author on a bestselling career in both main markets; likewise, Len Deighton's *The Ipcress File* (1962). Ken Follett's *Eye of the Needle* (1978; will a German spy contrive to smuggle the 'Overlord' invasion plan to his masters?) and Jack Higgins's *The Eagle Has Landed* (1974; German raid to kidnap Churchill) attracted huge subsidiary rights payments from the American paperback sector and sold massively in both markets. Frederick Forsyth's *The Day of the Jackal* (1971; assassination attempt on De Gaulle) established him as another of America's favourite (British) thriller writers. All the above inspired big-budget film adaptations; all but one by Hollywood.

Another bestselling category in which Britain could claim to lead was children's literature (for adults as well), with authors such as Roald Dahl, Richard Adams (*Watership Down*, 1973), Terry Pratchett, Philip Pullman, Sue Townsend, and J. K. Rowling.

'Quality fiction' writers were also enthusiastically taken up in America, sometimes before they made any mark in their home country. They would include John Fowles (*The Magus, The French Lieutenant's Woman, Daniel Martin*), D. M. Thomas (*The White Hotel*), and A. S. Byatt (*Possession*).

As with television comedy, British whimsy was often discovered to be to American taste, notably Douglas Adams's *Hitch-Hiker's Guide to the Galaxy* (1978), George MacDonald Fraser's witty and learned inverted-Victorian 'Flashman' (1969–) sequence, and updated Diaries of Nobodies, such as Nick Hornby's *High Fidelity* (1995: a successful, Americanized, film was made in 2000). Hornby's obsessively chart-devising Rob Gordon is a kind of human satire on bestseller lists.

At the turn of the century, the most successful genre writer in both the UK and the US was Ian Rankin, with his Edinburgh-based 'Rebus' police procedural. At one point, Rankin was credited with clearing 10% of all mass-market fiction in the UK. Rankin's supremely successful formula can be traced back to John Creasey's innovative, 20-strong 'Gideon of the Yard' series, which ran from the mid-1950s (with *Gideon's Day*, 1955) to the mid-1970s. The novels were issued under one of Creasey's many pen names,

J. J. Maric. Like Rebus, George Gideon is world-weary, morally exhausted – but none the less a crusader down the mean streets of his city: a holder of what Joseph Wambaugh (who conceived a similar series of police procedurals set in Los Angeles) called the 'thin blue line'.

British popular fiction: modern pattern(s)

At any point after the 1960s, British bestsellers comprise a quilt of styles, levels of literary quality, novels aimed at older or younger readers, and works originating alternately at home or away. Take, for example, the fiction bestsellers of 1960–5, as recorded by W. H. Smith:

1960
Clea, Lawrence Durrell
Return to Peyton Place, Grace Metalious
The Leopard, Giuseppe di Lampedusa
For Your Eyes Only, Ian Fleming

1961
A Burnt Out Case, Graham Greene
The Chapman Report, Irving Wallace
A Severed Head, Iris Murdoch
The Pale Horse, Agatha Christie

1962
Life at the Top, John Braine
The Pumpkin Eater, Penelope Mortimer
Youngblood Hawk, Herman Wouk
The Bull from the Sea, Mary Renault
Dead Cert, Dick Francis

1963
The Carpetbaggers, Harold Robbins
On Her Majesty's Secret Service, Ian Fleming
The Shoes of the Fisherman, Morris West
The Group, Mary McCarthy

1964

The Spy Who Came in from the Cold, John Le Carré

This Rough Magic, Mary Stewart

You Only Live Twice, Ian Fleming

1965

Corridors of Power, C. P. Snow

The Man with the Golden Gun, Ian Fleming

The Looking-Glass War, John Le Carré

An American Dream, Norman Mailer

It's a bag of nails. But running through it is a sustaining vein of middle-brow (and, one may suspect, middle-aged) solidity (Greene, Christie, Renault, Snow, Stewart, Francis) and a smaller, but still impressive, high-mindedness (Greene, Lampedusa). What seems missing, at this point in the 1960s, is any strong presence of a younger cohort of readers – it is where popular music had been ten years before: stuck, demographically, in the middle.

At any point, even until well into the new millennium, there is strong and growing congruence between the British and American lists, but never a perfect fit. The quilted pattern can be seen persisting in a parallel listing of the bestsellers of the last five years of the century, taken from the same source, W. H. Smith's annual round-ups of their bestselling titles:

1996

Appassionata, Jilly Cooper

Evening Class, Maeve Binchy

To The Hill, Dick Francis

Hogfather, Terry Pratchett

1997

Jingo, Terry Pratchett

The God of Small Things, Arundhati Roy

10-lb Penalty, Dick Francis

Birds of Prey, Wilbur Smith

1998

Charlotte Gray, Sebastian Faulks

Rainbow Six, Tom Clancy

Tara Road, Maeve Binchy

Point of Origin, Patricia Cornwell

1999

Hannibal, Thomas Harris

Bridget Jones: The Edge of Reason, Helen Fielding

Adrian Mole: The Cappuccino Years, Sue Townsend

The Fifth Elephant, Terry Pratchett

2000

The Bear and the Dragon, Tom Clancy

Scarlet Feather, Maeve Binchy

Shattered, Dick Francis

Winter Solstice, Rosamunde Pilcher

American blockbusters are prominent enough (Clancy, Cornwell, Harris) but so, too, are old favourites (Francis, now almost 40 years into his second career as jockey turned novelist) and romance (Binchy). There is also – notably – the impact of a younger-looking cohort: Helen Fielding's chick-lit princess, Bridget Jones; a post-adolescent (but still not 'grown-up') Adrian Mole, and the umpteenth instalment of Pratchett's Discworld sequence. Arundhati Roy's Booker-winning *The God of Small Things* testifies to the growing influence of literary prizes on fiction sales. The quilt's pattern is changing.

Recent technological advances mean that British bestsellers are, in the first decade of the 21st century, more accurately monitored, recorded, and analysed than at any period in history. The 2006 bestseller paperback lists drawn up in January 2007 indicate that, at the top of the market, the mix comprises heavyweight American imports (the unsinkable Brown), a strong romance component (Mosse and Hislop), and – with Lewycka's first novel – input from the Man Booker and other prizes which the novel either won, or was shortlisted for.

The Da Vinci Code, Dan Brown: 1,019,533
Labyrinth, Kate Mosse: 865,402
The Island, Victoria Hislop: 660,910
A Short History of Tractors in Ukrainian, Monica Lewycka: 631,898
Angels and Demons, Dan Brown: 589,761

One thing is clear from such lists, and from surveys of the field generally: the market for popular fiction continues to boom.

Bestsellers

Chapter 6
The future of the bestseller: is there one?

Digitization

Digitization has impacted on the entire arc of the book process: from the first stroke on the authorial keyboard, through computer typesetting, printing, and inventory control, to the electronic bookshop like Amazon, with its hourly updated bestseller lists. In the 'traditional' walk-in bookshop, POS (point-of-sale) monitoring allows finger-on-the-pulse feedback, which is constantly refining the demand, supply, and consumption cycle.

To the eye, the codex book looks the Caxtonish thing it always has. Black ink, white paper, hard/soft covers. But the machinery behind that familiar thing is half-a-millennium different.

In this digital mix one may also include fanzine activity. From www.stephenking.com to www.readthewest.com (i.e. the 'western'), no bestselling author, or line of fiction, will not nowadays have its authorized or non-authorized website – advertising, mobilizing, exegetizing the texts.

Bestsellers are increasingly subjects of attention on the blogosphere, with its blogcrit, blogbuzz, and bloghype. There are new web-based discussion boards, whose enthusiasms generate sales (or the opposite). Word of mouth – that most effective retail commodity – is now cyber-propelled and digitally supercharged.

The chip has changed the whole sociology and circuitry of traditional production and consumption – dependent as it used to be on the intermediaries of the print/placard advertisement, the review, the walk-in-browse-in bookshop, and the public library.

The electronic delivery chain has, over the last 20 years, substantially cheapened the product to the customer at the same time that the same customer has substantially more disposable income. This explains, in part, the inexorable growth in bestseller sales: both cumulatively and for individual titles.

Quite new, but very potent in this new ensemble, are the vast fanzine activities buzzing around, notably the Potter, Pullman, and Tolkien franchises. This can take the form of traditional commentary and discussion, or more adventurous exercises in fanfic – or adulatory composition – such as Cassandra Claire's homage to Tolkien, *The Very Secret Diaries*. Random blogbuzz has not yet 'made' a bestseller in the way, for example, that it did with the movie *The Blair Witch Project*, but one can be confident that it will, in the not too distant future.

Organized blogbuzz – the power of the electronic congregation – was most certainly responsible (via such websites as www.leftbehind.com and www.raptureready.com) for the extraordinary success of Tim La Haye and Jerry Jenkins and their *Left Behind* fictionalization of the Book of Revelation, intended to climax with the Second Coming and Final Judgement (the great reviewer in the sky will have his final say). The general readers' first reaction to the triumph of the *Left Behind* series was that of Butch Cassidy as he and Sundance are chased by the mysterious posse: 'Who *are* these guys?' Where did they come from? What was propelling the *Left Behind* phenomenon was less a readership, or 'fans' in the traditional sense, than a newfangled e-congregation. As the religious right, in alliance with new communications technology, had changed the face of American politics, and movie DVD consumption (with Mel Gibson's *The Passion of the Christ*), so the same combination was changing the field of mass motivations which drives the popular fiction industry.

The concurrent advance of web-selling (notably via Amazon) and the web-merchandiser's capacity for 'customizing' its clients' preferences suggested that the 'stampede' model of 20th-century consumption might be in the process of changing, rapidly and drastically. In the future, there will not be national bestsellers but 'group preferences' organized around web-connected readerships, supplied by web-retailers attentive to the group's taste. This is the optimistic 'long tail' thesis – a sophistication of the mechanisms of choice which will render the 'old-fashioned' bestseller, and its last-century machinery, obsolete. In the future, readers will increasingly refine (or mature) their preferences, and suppliers will increasingly profile and satisfy their idiosyncratic needs.

E-bestselling

There is a third component in this projected transformation: namely, the physical nature of the book itself. 'Who reads e-books?' asked a perplexed article in *USA Today* in 2004. 'Very few people – *yet*' was the answer. Huge amounts of money have been poured into the technology – notably by Sony, whose pioneer 'e-book' came on the market in 2005.

In the early phases of the new technology, a main problem was chaotic packaging: Adobe, Microsoft, Mobipocket, Palm – multi-format (open) or 'secure' (encrypted, non-copyable) versions. Another problem was the skittishness of publishers, nervous that digitized texts are so easy to pirate and bootleg. No one wanted to go back to the American 1880s.

Partly, too, there was resistance from the retail sector inhibiting innovative biblio-technology. E-books downloaded from the Web would circumvent the bookseller entirely. And partly, on the consumer's side, the inhibition arose from the sheer inconvenience of reading print in eye-bruising pixellated form. None the less, by 2006, e-merchandisers could claim that sales are increasing by 40% annually.

Who was buying? One's automatic reaction is that it must be the iPod generation – younger readers who have had electronic playthings since they were in the nursery. And mainly males – the gender that loves new technology.

What kind of book would young Mr Geek go for? Science fiction, of course. And it is true that there is a vibrant e-readership for SF (see the no-cost archive of e-SF, available at www.baen.com/library). But the real growth point was elsewhere, as Malle Vallik, an executive at Harlequin Books, reported in a summer 2006 bulletin of the Romance Writers of America:

> The myth is that the e-book reader is a techno-loving gadget-obsessed guy. But the typical e-book reader is much more likely to be a passionate reader who loves the instant gratification of downloading the book she wants to read and the ability to carry many titles with her ... The exciting news is that romance is the fastest-growing category in the e-book market.

There are two leading e-platforms for access to and information about e-books: the International Digital Publishing Forum (www.idpf.org) and Fictionwise (www.fictionwise.com). Both websites compile bestseller lists that bear out Ms Vallik's analysis. With e-books, women, it would seem, rule. It is the old story: it was women readers, in 18th-century England, who created the foundation for the rise of the novel.

E-fiction, specifically e-bestsellers, are not merely new technology – a superior delivery system – they will bring with them a new sociology of reading and consumption. A pattern which is less list- and more Web-driven, representing new mobilizations and communities of reader.

Reading, it is safe to prophesy, will survive and thrive. The appetite for on-page (whether paper or electronic) popular fiction looks to be as insatiable as it ever was. But within the new wholly digitized regime, the 'bestseller', as it was concocted in the hot-house of American bookselling in the late 19th century and perfected in the 20th century, will probably, at some not too distant point, join the internal combustion engine in the junkyard of history.

Further reading

Traditionally the 'Bibliography' attached to works like this is so much dead weight – there to validate the scholarly bona fides of the venture and the author, but typically of relatively little utility (compared, for instance, to a good index). Nowadays, particularly with a subject such as bestsellers, there is other practical advice to be given.

With the major novelists, for instance, and with many of the minor, there are useful websites – all easily located by Google.

There have been some serious and informative recent academic studies of bestsellers and Popular Fiction, notably Clive Bloom's *Bestsellers: Popular Fiction since 1990* (London, 2002: a monograph whose title flatteringly echoes my *Bestsellers: Popular Fiction of the 1970s*, London, 1981) and Ken Gelder's *Popular Fiction: The Logics and Practice of a Literary Field* (London, 2004). Theoretical as Professor Gelder's title sounds, his range of reference is, given the mind-boggling size of the subject he writes about, unusually extensive. His appendices include a comprehensive list of online resources.

John M. Unsworth, Dean and Professor of the Graduate School of Library and Information Science at the University of Illinois, Urbana-Champaign, runs a pioneering course in 20th-century

American bestsellers which hosts, on its website, authoritative lists and peripheral material. See http://www3.isrl.uiuc.edu/~unsworth/courses/bestsellers/. The website features a growing library of essays by students which are highly informative.

The problem of accurately identifying what bestsellers are – and, even more problematically, what they *were* in the past – is complex and will need preliminary explanation. A good account of the variability between lists is given at http://en.wikipedia.org/wiki/Bestseller. For the purpose of this Very Short Introduction, I have drawn mainly (for America) on the *New York Times* lists, particularly as summarized by Alice Payne Hackett, in her volume-form round-ups of those statistics: *70 Years of Best Sellers, 1895–1965* (New York, 1967) and *80 Years of Best Sellers, 1895–1975* (New York, 1977). *The Bowker Annual Library and Book Trade Almanac*, which has extraordinarily full statistical information from the 1950s onwards, is a valuable resource, as are Professor Unsworth's tables, appended on his website, and those similar tables available on www.caderbooks.com. In the UK, before formal bestseller lists made an appearance in the 1970s, one is obliged to fall back on such sources as W. H. Smith's annual round-ups. There is an inevitable statistical fuzziness. Since the early 1960s, as an individual project, Alex Hamilton laboriously assembled sales figures of British books whose summaries were published, annually, in the *Guardian* newspaper. They can be consulted on the paper's electronic archive.

The best account of the pre-20th-century bestseller is Frank Luther Mott's *Golden Multitudes: The Story of Best Sellers in the United States* (New York, 1947). Raymond Escarpit's *The Book Revolution* (London, 1966) is a classic work of literary sociology which offers a conceptual framework for the subject (Escarpit is particularly illuminating on the 'bestseller'/'fastseller' distinction). More inward with the modern American book trade is Michael Korda, *Making the List: A Cultural History of the American Bestseller, 1900–1999* (New York, 2001). John G.

115

Cawelti's *Adventure, Mystery and Romance* (Chicago, 1976) lays down a serviceable set of categories with which to make sense of bestsellers. Two of the wittiest books on the subject are Claud Cockburn's *Bestseller: The Books that Everyone Read, 1900–1939* (London, 1972) and Colin Watson's *Snobbery with Violence* (London, 1979).

In addition to citing the scholarship of Professor Unsworth and Professor Gelder I wish to further acknowledge my debt to them for having read, frequently corrected, and advised on my text. Their work has also held up a standard for my own to aspire to.

Index

Bestsellers

LITERARY THEORY
A Very Short Introduction
Jonathan Culler

Literary Theory is a controversial subject. Said to have transformed the study of culture and society in the past two decades, it is accused of undermining respect for tradition and truth, encouraging suspicion about the political and psychological implications of cultural products instead of admiration for great literature. In this Very Short Introduction, Jonathan Culler explains 'theory', not by describing warring 'schools' but by sketching key 'moves' that theory has encouraged and speaking directly about the implications of cultural theory for thinking about literature, about the power of language, and about human identity. This lucid introduction will be useful for anyone who has wondered what all the fuss is about or who wants to think about literature today.

> 'It is impossible to imagine a clearer treatment of the subject, or one that is, within the given limits of length, more comprehensive. Culler has always been remarkable for his expository skills, and here he has found exactly the right method and tone for his purposes.'
>
> **Frank Kermode**

www.oup.co.uk/vsi/literarytheory

POSTMODERNISM
A Very Short Introduction
Christopher Butler

Postmodernism has become the buzzword of contemporary society over the last decade. But how can it be defined? In this Very Short Introduction Christopher Butler lithely challenges and explores the key ideas of postmodernism, and their engagement with literature, the visual arts, film, architecture, and music. He treats artists, intellectuals, critics, and social scientists 'as if they were all members of a loosely constituted and quarrelsome political party' – a party which includes such members as Jacques Derrida, Salman Rushdie, Thomas Pynchon, David Bowie, and Micheal Craig-Martin – creating a vastly entertaining framework in which to unravel the mysteries of the 'postmodern condition', from the politicizing of museum culture to the cult of the politically correct.

> 'a preeminently sane, lucid, and concise statement about the central issues, the key examples, and the notorious derilections of postmodernism. I feel a fresh wind blowing away the miasma coiling around the topic.'
>
> **Ihab Hassan, University of Wisconsin, Milwaukee**

www.o